# Men and Battle
# Tigers Over Asia

A Talisman / Parrish Book

# TIGERS OVER ASIA

Bernard C. Nalty

**Elsevier-Dutton**
New York

ISBN: 0-525-93007-8

Published in the United States by E. P. Dutton,
a Division of Sequoia-Elsevier Publishing Company, Inc., New York
Published simultaneously in Canada by
Clarke, Irwin & Company Limited, Toronto and Vancouver

Art Direction: The Etheredges
Production: Stephen Konopka

Printed in the U.S.A.     First Edition
10 9 8 7 6 5 4 3 2 1

# Contents

# Preface

The story of the American Volunteer Group, the Flying Tigers, is in large measure the saga of Claire L. Chennault, who trained and led these men. Chennault's experience in pursuit aviation helped shape the tactics he prescribed for the group. The success of the Flying Tigers enabled him to gain approval for an aerial campaign to be fought in China by a full-fledged air force under his command. This organization, the Fourteenth Air Force, inherited the tactics and traditions of the American Volunteer Group.

Along with this heritage, the Fourteenth Air Force shared many of the problems that had plagued the Flying Tigers. The worst of these was a chronic shortage of supplies. This condition resulted from the realities of geography, the towering mountains that lay at the end of a 5,000-mile supply line.

The unpublished letters and reports that lend detail to this narrative became available through the generosity of Mr. Thomas Sturm, who is writing a book on the air defense of the United States, and Dr. John Greenwood, currently at work on a collection of correspondence between General Henry H. Arnold, Commanding General, U.S. Army Air Forces, during World War II, and his principal subordinates. Their assistance proved extremely valuable. Special thanks are due Major General John W. Huston, Chief of Air Force History, who read the manuscript and offered perceptive comment.

BERNARD C. NALTY

Flying Tigers—Curtiss P-40s with tiger shark markings

# 1. The Tigers Are Born

On 20 December 1941, telephones were ringing at the headquarters of the American Volunteer Group. Ten Japanese bombers, reported the most distant observation post, had just crossed the border of China's Yunnan Province. The group commander, Texas-born Claire L. Chennault, glanced through the window at the Curtiss P-40Bs, sharks' teeth painted on their noses, that stood on the parking area of the Kunming airfield.

Although his native country had been at war with Japan since the attack on Pearl Harbor, 13 days earlier, Chennault wore the uniform of the Chinese Air Force. Like the men who flew and maintained the P-40s and the other Americans operating the headquarters, he was serving the government of China. Besides commanding these volunteers, who called themselves the Flying Tigers, he was principal aviation adviser to Chiang Kai-shek, leader in China's battle against the invading Japanese.

As Chennault waited, other observation posts reported seeing or hearing the enemy formation. Gradually a course emerged on the plotting board at one end of the room. The planes, it was clear, were bound for a point some 50 miles east of Kunming, where they would select a final course to attack the city. Chennault fired a red flare that burst overhead. This signal sent 24 of his volunteer pilots dashing to their waiting aircraft.

1

Ed Rector crashed in a rice paddy but went on to become an ace

The Allison engines whined, then sputtered to life, and the fighters rolled onto the runway. Within a few minutes, if all went well, a formation of Flying Tigers, personally trained by Chennault to fight in teams, would intercept the unescorted Japanese bombers short of the intended target. At last China had a modern air force to protect its cities.

Chennault, along with Harvey Greenlaw, who served as his executive officer, and their interpreter, drove to a cemetery overlooking the airfield. There he entered an operations center that had been built by Chinese coolies. While the interpreter took telephone reports from observers on the ground, the two Americans listened to the radio chatter among the pilots, who were about to put Chennault's carefully devised tactics to their first test in combat against an enemy who was already earning a reputation for near invincibility.

The defensive plan called for "Scarsdale Jack" Newkirk, a native of that New York suburb, to intercept the enemy with four P-40s, while Jim Howard, whose parents had been missionaries in China, patrolled nearer Kunming with his four fighters, in case the bombers slipped past Newkirk. West of the city, Robert Sandell, a Texan, circled with 16 planes, serving as a reserve.

On the ground at Kunming, Chennault heard the babble of excited voices, then silence. Fearing the worst, he radioed Sandell to lead the reserve into action. Minutes later the telephone began jangling as Chinese observers reported that the bombers, now fewer in number, were fleeing toward Japanese bases in Indochina.

Howard's flight landed first. The men said that the enemy had not got through to their patrol area. Next came Newkirk's patrol. He and his men had spotted the Japanese cruising unescorted at 10,000 feet but simply could not believe their eyes. These Flying Tigers delayed for vital seconds, and instead of delivering coordinated attacks they broke formation, making long shallow dives that gave the intended victims plenty of time to react. Bombs screamed harmlessly earthward as the twin-engine aircraft came about and lowered their noses to gain speed. Far behind them, Newkirk's flight blazed away, though far out of range. One Tiger, Ed Rector, chased headlong after the enemy, inflicting no damage but running out of gas and crash-landing in a rice paddy. To Chennault, who had killed many a deer as a hunter in Louisiana, the reaction of Newkirk, Rector and the others was understandable: they had experienced a bad case of buck fever.

Before Rector had broken off his fruitless chase, Sandell's reserve had arrived overhead and immediately dived to the attack. Again the discipline preached by Chennault collapsed; teams never formed, and 16 individuals blazed away with little regard for range or deflection. Fritz Wolf, for instance, downed two bombers but discovered that he had shot up all his ammunition when he went after a third.

Although low on fuel, Sandell's patrol buzzed the field at Kunming and executed victory rolls. As soon as the men had landed and emerged from their machines, they gathered around Chennault, pouring out stories of burning bombers and jammed guns. But the commander wasn't handing out any medals. He led his men into one of the buildings, patiently sorted out what had happened, and explained the mistakes they had made. Next time out, the Flying Tigers would be better disciplined and even deadlier. The sky would no longer be the private property of the Japanese.

# 2. Claire Chennault- American Airman

Claire Lee Chennault, the retired U.S. Army air officer who trained and led the Flying Tigers, was born at Commerce, Tex., in 1890 and spent his boyhood in northeastern Louisiana. His mother died when he was five years old, and his father, John Stonewall Chennault, taught him to hunt and fish, essential skills in that impoverished corner of the state. He remained an outdoorsman for the rest of his life.

The elder Chennault remarried when Claire was 10. Unlike the stepmothers of legend, Lottie Barnes Chennault, a teacher, was devoted to Claire, a feeling that he returned. She encouraged his outdoor activity but also helped him become interested in school work.

To young Chennault, life was a succession of challenges. He felt he had to rank first in his studies and lead the way on the athletic field. Merely making the team was not enough; he had to pitch for the baseball squad, play quarter back in football, and be the center in basketball. He was a leader, worshipped by younger children but disliked—and with some justification—by the older boys. In his autobiography, *Way of a Fighter,* he recalled that he was shy around older persons, easily angered by criticism and reluctant to reveal his thoughts, feelings or hopes.

His experience in hunting and fishing had bred in him a certain re-

5

sourcefulness and self-confidence, so that he did his best work when left entirely on his own. His mind was quick and retentive, but he hated to explain anything more than once. When questioned closely, he tended to become defensive, a trait that stayed with him and plagued him during his military career.

That career began at Louisiana State University, which had mandatory military training complete with the hazing of first-year students. Assigned to stand guard in front of the entrance to the dining hall, 14-year-old Cadet Chennault fixed bayonet to rifle, shouldered the weapon and paced back and forth. From a balcony above, upperclassmen dumped pitchers of water on him, but he did not break stride. Then mess call sounded, and Claire had his revenge. While the food—probably not too appetizing to begin with—grew cold, he held the older students at bayonet point until they could find the cadet officer of the day. Not until he had been relieved of his post did Chennault allow anyone to pass. At this time, although so young, he was enrolled in the school of agriculture, the only branch of the university that would accept him.

Since he had no real interest in any particular professional training, an officer's career seemed attractive, so he applied at both service academies. He went to Annapolis to take the Naval Academy entrance examination, a three-day ordeal. After the second day he heard someone say that midshipmen were confined to the academy grounds for their first two years, and his outdoorsman's instincts rebelled. Convinced that academy life was not for him he returned to rural Louisiana.

He next tried his hand at teaching. After obtaining a certificate from a state teachers' college, he got a job at Athens, La. He proved to be exactly what the local school board wanted—tough, willing to work cheap, and legally a minor who could beat up his unruly pupils without risking a charge of assault and battery. Here, too, his determination to excel showed itself. He not only pounded the biggest of his students into submission but also organized and coached an undefeated baseball team.

Although Chennault enjoyed teaching in this country school, he soon discovered he could not live on the salary he was receiving. Marriage to Nell Thompson on Christmas Day, 1911, and the birth of the first two of their eight children sent him scrambling from job to job, teaching at a variety of schools and eventually ending up as a laborer in an Akron, Ohio, factory.

He was working there in April 1917, when the United States declared war on Germany. He immediately applied for flight training but at 26 was rejected for being too old and for having too many dependents—a wife and by this time three children. The Army did, however, accept him for the infantry and assigned him to a three-month officer training course. His first assignment after graduation took him to Fort Travis, on the opposite side of San Antonio, Tex., from the pilot training center at Kelly Field. Still fascinated by the idea of flying, which seemed a greater challenge than leading foot soldiers, Chennault volunteered to serve at the aviation school. Acceptance came swiftly enough, but instead of learning to fly he spent his time meeting prospective air cadets at the railroad station and marching them to the airfield.

Despite this disappointing assignment, Chennault proved equal to this latest self-generated challenge. During the year spent at Kelly Field, he persuaded some of the instructors to give him flying lessons. Then he talked himself into a job as an engineering officer at a satellite field where his only responsibilities were to fuel the planes and keep track who was flying which wood-and-fabric Curtiss Jenny biplane. As he had anticipated, he found plenty of time for solo flights.

In the fall of 1918, as the war was rushing to a climax, Chennault received orders to Mitchel Field, Long Island, where he became nonflying adjutant of the 46th Pursuit Squadron. Late in October the unit packed up and marched to Garden City, N.Y., for the train ride to New York City, where a ship waited to carry it to France. Halfway to Garden City the column reversed direction and trudged back to Mitchel Field. No further aviation units were needed overseas.

Before boredom had settled in, word reached Mitchel Field that some 350 miles to the south the black construction troops building Langley Field, Va., were on the brink of mutiny. Serenely confident that white southerners could best deal with angry blacks, the War Department called upon Chennault and others of similar background to restore order at Langley. He arrived to find that this crisis was more imagined than real, but soon a genuine danger appeared.

While Chennault was at Langley Field, the great Spanish influenza epidemic struck, felling men by the hundreds. Hangars became hospitals, as the sick list lengthened, and Chennault was put in charge of one of these makeshift wards. Then he, too, became a victim of the disease. His condition worsened until two litter bearers, their faces covered with surgical masks to avoid contagion, carried him to a shed that had become an anteroom to the morgue.

Abandoned to die, Chennault was lying there when the assistant provost marshal, who had given him unauthorized flying lessons at Kelly Field, discovered him. The older officer forced him to drink from a bottle of bourbon confiscated from smugglers who had defied the wartime prohibition law. Chennault downed the entire quart over the space of a few days and, amazingly, regained his health. He always credited the whiskey with saving his life.

Having survived the flu, Chennault now faced the perils of flight training, for orders summoned him back to Kelly as an air cadet. At last he was soaring through the sky in the familiar two-place Jenny with dual controls. In some 80 hours aloft, he had acquired some bad habits that infuriated his

7

instructor, a civilian named Pop Likens. Teacher resembled pupil: Likens, too, hated to make explanations; when anything went wrong, he wrapped both hands around the control stick in his cockpit and yanked the airplane out of the cadet's hands. After undergoing this humiliation a few times, Chennault vowed that if Likens again grabbed the controls he would refuse to take them back.

The next time the two went up, after Chennault had throttled back and was gliding toward a cornfield, practicing emergency landings, Likens again lost patience and abruptly took over. True to his word, Chennault refused to take the stick back. The biplane wallowed on the brink of a stall before Likens realized the Curtiss was flying itself. The instructor dropped the nose and gathered speed, skimming the corn tassels as he pulled up. Safely back at Kelly Field, the furious instructor stormed into the operations section and demanded that Chennault be washed out of flight training.

But before being dismissed from the program, every cadet got a second chance—another flight with a different instructor. Luckily, Chennault drew Ernest Allison, another civilian, who proved as easygoing as Likens was volatile. Allison not only gave Chennault a passing grade but also introduced him to aerobatics, showing him how to kick the Jenny around like a fighter plane.

Early in 1919, Chennault graduated with the rating of pursuit pilot and received his separation papers from the Army. He promptly applied for a regular commission in the Air Service, which he received in the spring of 1920. From the family farm in Louisiana he headed for Ellington Field, Tex., and the 94th Pursuit Squadron of the 1st Pursuit Group.

At Ellington Field, Chennault perfected the aerobatic skills that Ernest Allison had demonstrated for him during the "wash-out ride." With two other young pilots, Joe Cannon and Don Stace, he tried to improve the dogfighting tactics that had evolved during World War I. One of their experiments, however, almost ended in tragedy. Instead of automatically rolling into a dive when jumped from the rear, Chennault suggested a half loop with a rollout at the top, a variation on the wartime Immelmann turn. Cannon, flying a British-designed SE-5, offered to test Chennault's idea by attacking Stace's French Spad.

As the SE-5 knifed downward, Stace entered the loop, lost momentum and fell off on one wing. Intent on duplicating the Immelmann turn, Cannon collided with the slow-moving Spad, and both planes plunged earthward. Stace succeeded in recovering from a tight spin and landing safely. Not having a parachute—a rare piece of equipment in those days— Cannon had no choice but to stay with his crippled SE-5, which raised a pall of dust when it struck but did not burn.

Chennault, in another Spad, dived low over the wreckage, saw no sign of life and returned to Ellington to dispatch an ambulance, though a hearse

Claire Lee Chennault as commander of the
Fourteenth Air Force, 1944

actually seemed more appropriate. When the vehicle arrived at the crash scene, Cannon was waiting, miraculously alive, though his jaw and some ribs were broken and his face a maze of cuts. He survived to hold important commands during World War II and in the Korean conflict.

A few years later, while in Hawaii with the 19th Pursuit Squadron, Chennault introduced another innovation—having a three-plane element maneuver as a team to provide mutual support and protection. The wingmen not only reinforced their leader's fire but also covered his rear. Although most pilots in Chennault's squadron were wary of tight formations, he persuaded them to try the new tactics. At first their maneuvers were tentative, but they soon became more precise, as the pilots became enthusiastic converts to Chennault's theories. During the 1925 Army-Navy war games, when a Navy scout bomber unit passed overhead in the opposite direction, Chennault signaled for a simultaneous half loop and roll that brought the entire squadron into position to attack the other formation from behind. Years later he declared that the sudden maneuver had caused an astonished naval aviator to lose control of his plane and flop down on the surface of Pearl Harbor.

Besides pursuing his interest in team tactics, Chennault used the 1925 war games to experiment with air-raid warning. He issued binoculars to two enlisted men and posted them atop the Luke Field water tower with the mission of spotting aircraft approaching Ford Island, where the airfield was located. This crude peacetime method, which barely gave Chennault's MB-3 biplanes warning enough to get into the air and greet the Navy attackers, marked the beginning of an idea that would prove decisive in wartime China.

In 1931 Chennault reported to the Air Corps Tactical School, where he found Clayton Bissell, a World War I ace, teaching fighter tactics. In those days students had to put into practical use whatever they had learned from lectures and map exercises by climbing into the different kinds of aircraft and flying practice missions. Bissell taught the younger pilots to do what he had done so skillfully over the Western Front—to fly area patrols during which they searched for enemy aircraft, tried to dive upon them out of the sun, and fought plane against plane.

Chennault, however, disagreed with these traditional tactics, arguing that a person might as well send sparrows after hawks. Unless defending pursuit pilots knew the general course being followed by the attacking bombers, they would waste precious time and fuel searching out the marauders and might fail to make contact. No wonder that enthusiasts like Kenneth Walker believed their new monoplane bombers, faster than most pursuits, were all but invulnerable.

After graduating, Chennault stayed on as an instructor, moving with the Tactical School from Langley Field to Maxwell Field, Ala. He took advantage of this new assignment to challenge traditional fighter doctrine in a

General "Hap" Arnold (l.) once asked, "Who is this damned fellow Chennault?"

mimeographed textbook, *The Role of Defensive Pursuit*. Challenging tradition in this fashion was not at all unusual. In the words of one of Chennault's students, "this Tactical School was not a place where a guy stood up and said: This is Gospel, take it or leave it. . . . It was a place in which the students would also put the instructors on the griddle. It was an intellectual symposium, that's what it was."

In this climate, Chennault announced that he did not agree with the principle that "bombardment, once in the air, cannot be stopped," a point of view then being pushed by many of his fellow Air Corps officers and, Chennault said, by many "European leaders." He pointed out that those who preached the invincibility of the bomber were forgetting "the ancient principle that 'for every new weapon there is an effective counter weapon.'" For Chennault that counter weapon was the pursuit plane. Properly employed, he said, it could intercept and destroy the approaching bomber.

Chennault's textbook outlined the tactics the Flying Tigers would use in China. "Successful air defense," he wrote, consists of three phases of operations: "(1) detecting and reporting; (2) interception by pursuit; and (3) destruction or repulse of the invaders . . ." At this time Chennault was emphasizing the first point, detection. He proposed a network of ground reporting stations, possibly supplemented by aerial pickets, that could track the bombers during both approach and withdrawal. The pursuit

**11**

Stunt fliers John Williamson (l.), Chennault and William McDonald

planes, he argued, should remain on the ground until the operations center had worked out a likely point of interception. As the defending aircraft headed toward this point, a radio operator at the operations center relayed to them the information he was receiving from ground observers, thus enabling the flight to adjust its course to meet the enemy before he reached the intended target. Emergency signals, such as return to base, could be passed by means of large cloth panels displayed on the ground.

The Air Corps tested the underlying principles of the Chennault system during joint maneuvers with the antiaircraft artillery in the spring of 1933. To defend Fort Knox, Ky., from attack by new Boeing B-9 monoplanes and obsolete Curtiss and Keystone biplanes, the pursuit force employed a series of warning outposts scattered throughout a fan-shaped area extending some 60 miles from the target. But in practice this network failed to provide adequate warning. The interval between reporting stations proved too great, permitting the bombers to make frequent undetected course changes, and some observers were so close to Fort Knox that a few Curtiss P-6s or Boeing P-12s had to be sent to each of several possible interception points to prevent the bombers from slipping past unchallenged.

This one experiment did not shake Chennault's confidence, as was shown by his critique of a report prepared by Lieutenant Colonel Henry H. ("Hap") Arnold on an aerial war game staged on the West Coast during 1934. Arnold insisted that the lesson to be learned from these maneuvers was that pursuit planes would be ineffectual in wartime against modern bombers. Chennault, however, took sharp exception for several reasons.

First off, the Martin B-12 bombers making the mock attacks were the most modern aircraft of their type in the entire world, faster in level flight than the obsolescent P-26s trying to intercept them. In addition, the ground reporting posts again were too far apart, and the persons manning them had no optical equipment for determining the altitude of the bomber formation. As a result, the altitudes passed on to the pursuit pilots were all but meaningless—high, intermediate or low—a kind of terminology that Chennault compared to reporting an infantry division as "a large body of soldiers, most of whom are walking."

He leveled his strongest criticism at the sluggish fashion in which the P-26s had taken to the air. One unit had required nine minutes to become airborne after receiving orders to take off. Another had spent 23 minutes taking off, forming up and climbing to 15,000 feet. But no time should be wasted assembling an entire squadron in precise formation, Chennault declared; the objective was to gain altitude quickly. If necessary, pursuit pilots should attack the bombers from beneath rather than climb still higher to dive upon them.

Chennault also took exception to a recommendation, based on the results of the 1934 maneuvers, that the Air Corps acquire a large, multi-seat fighter with firepower equal to that of a bomber. Chennault argued that no plane this heavy could possibly fly faster than a bomber. What fighter pilots needed, he believed, was a single-seater faster than the P-26 and armed with 25-mm or 37-mm cannon instead of the usual pair of machine guns.

One of the opinions he expressed in the critique proved unsound, however. In stressing the need to break up the bomber formation, Chennault suggested that light bombs dropped from above by pursuit planes might force the bombers to scatter. During World War II, German airmen would try this gambit, with little success, against American B-17s and B-24s.

The critique caught the attention of Hap Arnold, who would become Commanding General, U.S. Army Air Forces, in the fight against the Axis powers. "Who is this damned fellow Chennault?" he asked his friends at the Air Corps Tactical School.

An officer enrolled in the school at the time has described the debate triggered by Chennault's comments on the Arnold report. "Now it was an unhappy situation," the officer recalled, "because the bombardment people were saying one thing, the attack people another, and Chennault was saying something else. Now something had to give. . . . And with the prevailing attitude of the time, especially when the B-10 would go faster than any pursuit ship we had, no question about who was going to win that argument."

In a rough-and-tumble debate characteristic of the Tactical School, the specialists in attack aviation, who bombed and strafed from low altitude, finally sided with the bombardment people, who dropped their explosives from high altitude, and together "they . . . just got Chennault where he was really being silly, really overreacting." He hated this criticism almost as much as he had detested being ridiculed by older boys during his Louisiana childhood.

Candor gave way to bitterness, as Chennault argued for what he believed. "He was contentious," an eyewitness reported. "His attitude was defensive. He was like a man with an inferiority complex, lashing out."

A decade later, in dictating his autobiography, Chennault complained bitterly about the "bomber boys who controlled the development of the Air Corps at the time," blaming their failure to develop long-range escort fighters for "the deaths of thousands of American boys who had been indoctrinated in the absolutely false theory that a bomber needs no protection from hostile fighters." The passage of time had not dulled his anger.

The quarrel triggered by his critique of the report of the West Coast war games generated ill feeling that ended his usefulness as an instructor of tactics, but his skill as a pilot remained undiminished. When the commandant of the Tactical School, Major General John F. Curry, saw a Navy precision flying team in action and vowed that his own airmen could do anything the sailors could, he turned to Chennault. Curry, in fact, formed his three-man team by turning Chennault loose in a P-12 and calling for volunteers to try to stay on his wing as he all but turned the biplane inside out. Three persons passed the test: Sergeant John H. ("Luke") Williamson and Second Lieutenant Haywood ("Possum") Hansell, who with Chennault formed the team, and Sergeant William McDonald, who became Hansell's replacement.

The night after their first performance at an air show, Chennault, Williamson and Hansell were celebrating their success in a Macon, Miss., barroom. After a few drinks, they began singing some old ballads, among them "The Daring Young Man on the Flying Trapeze," a song that inspired them to adopt the title "Three Men on a Flying Trapeze." The trio, their wing tips often no more than three feet apart, whipped through a dazzling series of maneuevers during their performances, but only once did they have an accident. While they were practicing over Chennault's home at Montgomery, Ala., with his wife watching, a wind gust forced Hansell's wing into Chennault's rudder, jamming the control stick. Without benefit of ailerons, elevators or rudder, Chennault managed to bring his plane safely down, using the throttle to control his approach and landing.

Hansell was the first to leave the group, being reassigned to other duties. Then in 1935, Williamson and McDonald failed to receive regular

In action: Three Men on a Flying Trapeze

commissions and decided to leave the Air Corps. Early in 1936, at an air show in Miami the team performed for the last time. Among those watching the intricate maneuvers was General Mow Pang Tsu (Mao Pang-tso) of the Chinese Air Force, who would figure prominently in Chennault's future.

At the time, however, Chennault did not seem to have much of a future; within a year of the Miami air show, his career had apparently reached a dead end. His aerobatic team had disbanded, his five years on the faculty of the Air Corps Tactical School had ended amid quarrels and fruitless controversy, and increasing deafness was causing problems. A flight surgeon barred him from flying anything faster than a training plane, and he could not even do that unless he was accompanied by a copilot. In January 1937 he was resting in the hospital at Barksdale Field, La., permanently grounded because of chronic bronchitis, low blood pressure and exhaustion. He was contemplating a civilian job, probably one that would put him behind a desk in the offices of some airplane manufacturer. Then came a letter from China that changed his life.

# 3. Adviser to Chiang Kai-shek

Roy Holbrook, an old friend and former fellow Air Corps pilot, had become an adviser to the Chinese government in its effort to build up its military strength. Now he extended an invitation that Chennault could not refuse. Mme. Chiang Kai-shek, he wrote, wanted Chennault to spend three months making a confidential inspection of China's air force. His salary would be $1,000 per month, plus expenses; he could go where he wished and fly any type of aircraft. Chennault, now retired from the Air Corps, accepted the offer immediately, moved his family to a Louisiana town called Waterproof, and headed for the Far East.

Chennault already knew in general what was happening in China. After the final performance of the Three Men on a Flying Trapeze, Holbrook had asked him to recommend American pilots to serve as instructors at Hangchow, the Chinese equivalent of Kelly Field. His two wingmen, Luke Williamson and Billy McDonald, seemed logical choices, Holbrook agreed, and both men signed contracts. From time to time Chennault received letters from them that revealed the desperate condition of China's air arm.

At any moment, the Japanese might renew the war that had started in 1931 and advance deeply into China. If the attack should come immedi-

Chennault with Chiang Kai-shek

ately, the Chinese Air Force would be ill prepared to resist. The Hang-chow flying school was torn by dissension, as an Italian training mission tried to supplant the Americans Holbrook had recruited. McDonald and the others complained that graft was rampant throughout the service, but reform seemed likely since Mme. Chiang was appointing an American as confidential inspector. Probing the condition of the Chinese Air Force promised to be as tough a challenge as Chennault had ever faced.

Upon receiving Chennault's message of acceptance, Mme. Chiang arranged for him to be met in Japan by Billy McDonald. Because a man engaged in training Chinese aviators would obviously be unwelcome in Japan, McDonald carried papers identifying him as the assistant manager of a Chinese acrobatic troop that was touring the country. He stayed for a time with the dancers and tumblers, then headed for Kobe, where Chennault's ship had docked. The two men visited Kyoto and Osaka—"flimsy heaps," according to Chennault—and traveled the Inland Sea looking for likely places to attack shipping. Although they took pictures and made notes on possible targets, gathering intelligence was a secondary activity. The main purpose of their tour was to give McDonald time to explain the complicated situation in the Far East.

By the time the two reached Shanghai in northern China, Chennault had become thoroughly familiar with the events of the past decade. In 1927, when Chiang Kai-shek's Kuomintang or Nationalist movement had been making headway against the entrenched foreign interests, Japan had become alarmed at the prospect of a unified China and had resumed meddling in Chinese internal affairs. Troops went ashore at Tsinan, ostensibly to protect the Japanese living there but actually to check the Nationalist advance toward Peking. Since Chiang was in the midst of a campaign to purge both Chinese and Russian Communists from the Kuomintang, he could not afford to antagonize the Japanese until he had achieved political unity and trained a modern army capable of defeating them.

In Manchuria, China's northernmost province, Marshal Chang Hsueh-liang, whose father had ruled as a Japanese puppet, turned against his masters. The Japanese reacted by detonating a bomb on the South Manchurian Railway near Mukden, blaming this "attack" on the Chinese, and seizing control of the province. During the fall and winter of 1931, Japan consolidated its control over Manchuria and early the following year incorporated it into the puppet state of Manchukuo. Japanese troops also probed south of the Great Wall, forcing Nationalist armies to withdraw from Tientsin, and landed at Shanghai, where the United States and Great Britain shared control over the International Settlement, while France maintained a separate concession nearby.

In December 1936, about the time that Chennault had entered the hospital at Barksdale Field, Chang Hsueh-liang tried a desperate gamble to rally all China against the Japanese. Throughout the conquest of Manchuria, Chiang Kai-shek had been preoccupied with destroying Mao Tsetung's Communists, and even now he was planning another campaign of extermination against them. When Chiang arrived in Sian province to enlist Chang's army in the offensive, the young marshal arrested his distinguished guest, vowing to hold him in custody until he agreed to form a united front with the Communists in opposing the conquerors of Manchuria.

Although Chang Hsueh-liang's bold action seemed to Mao's advantage, the Chinese Communists responded to Russian pressure and urged the release of their enemy. At the time the Soviet Union was anticipating Japanese activity along the border with Manchukuo and feared that Chiang's death or humiliation would deprive China of a leader whom Japan respected; Russian self-interest had triumphed over Communist solidarity. Chiang Kai-shek went free after tacitly agreeing to call off the planned campaign against Mao and to collaborate with him against the common foe. In reality, however, the two men were biding their time until the Japanese threat ended and they could decide the future of China. The kidnapping ended with Chiang Kai-Shek being hailed, at least by the western democracies, as a symbol of resistance against Japan and Chang Hseuh-liang under house arrest.

When Chennault arrived at Shanghai late in the spring of 1937, an uneasy truce prevailed throughout North China. The Japanese troops stationed at the city were roughly 200 miles from Chiang's capital of Nanking. An ominous sign that Japan might push deeper into China and try to play a larger role in world affairs was the signing in 1936 of the Anti-Comintern Pact, which bound Japan, Nazi Germany and Fascist Italy to oppose the spread of international Communism. The democratic nations had failed to prevent Hitler's Germany from reoccupying the demilitarized Rhineland and had proved ineffectual in the face of Italian aggression against Ethiopia. Was Japan now ready to ignore the opinion of the western democracies and resume hostilities in China?

Waiting at Shanghai for Chennault were Roy Holbrook, whose letter had brought the retired captain to the Orient, and W. H. Donald, an Australian newspaperman who had advised Chang Hsueh-liang to break with the Japanese. Impressed with this foreigner who had helped bring about Chang's conversion from opium addict and puppet to Chinese patriot, Chiang Kai-shek had recruited Donald. Prior to the kidnapping incident, the Australian had become Chiang's principal military adviser.

Whether advising Chang Hsueh-liang or Chiang Kai-shek, Donald stressed two things. One was honesty. He ferreted out and reported instances of corruption—commanders who either submitted pay vouchers for nonexistent troops or pocketed the money sent by the central government to pay real ones. Graft, however, was ingrained in Chinese life. Nor could Chiang have brought about reform even if he had chosen to do so. Although he bore the title of Generalissimo, he was by no means a supreme commander. Instead, he rested uneasily atop a pyramid of warlords and generals whose support he needed to remain in power. He dared not initiate any policy that might alienate them, even if that meant turning a blind eye to their corrupt activity.

Donald's other passion was aviation. While in Manchuria, he had persuaded Chang Hsueh-liang to purchase a twin-engine transport fitted out as an office. The marshal, who sometimes piloted the craft, flew throughout his province trying to rally his troops against the Japanese. In rugged areas where the plane could not land, soldiers either spread out prearranged signal panels to report the situation on the ground or lay on the ground to form characters that could be read from the air. All of this rushing about had failed, however, to save Manchuria. Indeed, the American military attaché in China, Colonel Joseph W. Stilwell, complained that Chang, instead of leading his troops in battle, spent all his time flying around in his airplane.

In Donald's opinion, aviation could do infinitely more for Chiang Kai-shek than it had for Chang Hsueh-liang. Obviously, China needed an air force for the inevitable showdown with Japan, but to be really effective this branch of service had to be under Chiang's direct control. The Nationalist leader had to be able to employ his aircraft as he desired, without having to work through some avaricious warlord.

Before leaving Shanghai, Chennault met Mme. Chiang, who resembled his idea of a fairy-tale princess, though she exuded energy and enthusiasm as well as charm. Upset by mismanagement and corruption within the fledgling air service, she asked Chennault, in her precise English, to begin his inspection immediately. He agreed, assuring her that he could complete the task within the specified three months.

Chennault soon came face to face with the realities of Chinese politics. He discovered, for example, that many of Chiang's pilots had defected from the air arm of one of the warlords, and could easily change allegiance once again, and that loyalty to Chiang or social status—not merit—often dictated who would graduate from flight training. As if these problems were not enough, the Nationalists had come to depend for military advice on Germany and Italy, Japan's partners in the Anti-Comintern Pact.

Although a cadre of thoroughly professional German officers provided sound advice on ground warfare, the Italian air mission seemed so inept that Chennault concluded that these men were sabotaging the Chinese Air Force. The Italians not only had introduced aircraft inferior to American types but also operated a flying school that automatically awarded wings to everyone who survived the training. Because no one failed the Italian course, the powerful families whose sons and nephews had enrolled never had to fear embarrassment, and Chiang was spared the problem of trying to explain how relatives of his supporters had failed the course. Unfortunately, the Italian methods also assured an endless supply of incompetent pilots.

Chennault also found corroboration for Mme. Chiang's charges of graft within the Air Force. The Chinese Aero Commission, which supervised this service, raised money by urging patriotic citizens to make contributions for the purchase of aircraft named for their home towns. The commissioners had a bomber flown from city to city, took up a collection at each stop and dutifully rechristened the machine each time—but apparently they pocketed the cash themselves. The actual number of combat-ready aircraft hovered around 100, although the commissioners listed 500 on their rolls.

The tour of inspection lasted only one month instead of three, for on 7 July 1937 the Japanese attacked Chinese forces at the Marco Polo Bridge, near Peking. Convinced that the struggle for China marked the prelude to a war between Japan and the United States, Chennault volunteered his services, and Chiang accepted, assigning him to a combat training school at Hangchow. This did not turn out to be one of Chennault's happier experiences. The food was not much to his liking, and the weather consisted of alternating dust storms and thundershowers. The commanding officer, the same General Mow who had seen the Three Men on a Flying Trapeze perform at Miami, turned out to be a skilled aviator, honest and hard working, but the task facing him was formidable. Except for a squadron of export

**20**

Chinese airfield builders haul rocks from nearby hills

versions of the Boeing P-26, the aircraft were inferior to Japanese types, and most of the pilots were Italian-trained and hopeless. As a result, Chennault remembered his time at Hangchow as a nightmare, characterized by as many as five crashes in a single day.

Meanwhile, Chiang was coming under intense pressure to take the fight to the Japanese. Perhaps the air was the answer. The Generalissimo summoned Mow and Chennault to his temporary headquarters, where he asked them if the air force was ready for battle. The answer was an unequivocal "No." Mow, thoroughly frightened, revealed that his combatready aircraft totaled only about one-fifth the number reported by the Aero Commission. The news infuriated Chiang, who threatened to have Mow shot. Mme. Chiang, who also was present, interpreted the Generalissimo's words and asked Chennault what he had learned during his abbreviated inspection tour. The American declared that Mow was absolutely right.

Chennault could not understand the torrent of Chinese that followed—Mme. Chiang made no attempt to translate—but he recognized that Chiang was trembling in wrath, the angriest he would see him during an association that lasted 10 years. This meeting not only sealed the doom of the Aero Commission but made Chennault one of the Generalissimo's most trusted advisers. As much as he hated to rely on foreigners, Chiang realized that Chennault, like Donald, was honest, able and loyal. The emergence of the American later proved especially fortunate for the Na-

21

Much of the Chinese air war was fought over rugged terrain

tionalist leader because Donald, visiting in the Philippines in 1941 when the Japanese invaded, would spend more than three years in an internment camp.

The revelations concerning the status of his air arm shook Chiang, who already knew that his goose-stepping German-trained army was no match for the more numerous and better equipped Japanese. His instincts told him to stall for time, but neither the warlords nor the educated classes would tolerate inaction. During a series of conferences at Nanking, which Chennault attended, the various generals pledged their support if the Generalissimo would fight. The unity Chiang had sought seemed to have arrived; he agreed to lead the struggle against Japan.

When a Japanese expedition attacked the Chinese at Shanghai, Mme. Chiang asked Chennault to plan an air strike on enemy shipping in the Whangpoo River, for none of General Mow's staff officers had ever attempted anything so complex. Chennault undertook the task, even though he had only Curtiss Hawk III biplane fighters and Northrop 2EC single-engine light bombers. The few surviving Heinkel 111A twin-engine medium bombers, bought from Germany, were not available, nor were the faster Martin 139s, export versions of the U.S. Army Air Corps B-10.

He decided to send the streamlined Northrop monoplanes against the cruiser *Idzumo*, which served as Japanese command post, while the Hawks dive-bombed other ships in the river. The hurriedly trained Northrop crews knew nothing about adjusting a bomb sight; the pilot maintained an altitude of 7,500 feet and a prescribed speed, while the bombardier sighted through a window in the belly of the plane, releasing his bombs when he saw the aiming picture he had memorized. To prevent an international incident, Chennault instructed the Chinese airmen to avoid those parts of Shanghai administered by the western powers.

On the day of the raid, a layer of cloud obscured the Shanghai area. With more courage than skill, the pilots dived through the overcast until they spotted their prey, then roared directly over the International Settlement as they headed for the cruiser. Unfortunately, the bombardiers did not realize they had to compensate for the change from the planned altitude. As a result, the *Idzumo* escaped damage, but one 1,100-pound bomb detonated in Nanking Road, one of the settlement's busiest streets. An estimated 1,000 Chinese died because of the explosion, and another 1,000 were wounded.

Following this tragic accident, Chennault climbed into a Curtiss Hawk 75, export version of the U.S. Army's P-36, and flew to Shanghai to observe Mow's airmen in action. He saw three Chinese planes diving on a large ship that was laying down a smoke screen and taking evasive action. Into the smoke he dived, skimming low over the afterdeck, upon which the crew had painted a huge Union Jack, and he had to bolt for safety as the British gunners opened fire. He saw once again that courage rather than skill was typical of the Chinese Air Force.

In the meantime, Chennault had set up a warning network that incorporated the lessons learned during the Fort Knox maneuver of four years earlier. Using existing telephone and telegraph lines, he tied in a series of observation posts throughout the Nanking-Shanghai-Hangchow area to warn of bombers approaching either Nanking, Chiang's capital, or the flying field at Hangchow. As Chennault deployed the warning net, Billy McDonald tried to teach the Chinese pursuit pilots a simple form of team tactics, instructing three men to concentrate on a single bomber, one attacking from above and another from below, while a third hovered to the rear until time for the kill.

The Japanese promptly tested these hastily organized defenses, sending 18 twin-engine Mitsubishi G3M2 bombers to hit the Hangchow air base. The defending Hawk IIIs received ample warning and were aloft when the enemy arrived, screened by clouds from these waiting interceptors. While the Curtiss fighters groped for the enemy, he bombed the vacant airfield and headed back to Formosa, the Japanese name for Taiwan. After the Japanese had reversed course, they emerged from the overcast. Now the Chinese could see them. The Hawks immediately attacked, shooting down between three and six bombers.

Following this setback, the Japanese went after Nanking, launching three unescorted daylight attacks in five days. Chennault claimed the destruction of at least 40 bombers, an estimate based on wreckage located by Chinese peasants. The Imperial Japanese Navy, defeated in its first aerial

**23**

offensive, concluded that further unescorted daylight bombing would be foolish and sent to Japan for protective fighters.

Until these aircraft arrived, the enemy tried night bombing. Observers on the ground listened for the drone of engines, watched for the flame from engine exhaust stacks, and reported the course the bombers were following toward Nanking. The capital's defenders used tactics that Chennault had worked out with General Wong, a German-trained artilleryman. While Wong's searchlight crews tracked the bombers, a handful of Mow's best pilots attacked, remaining just outside the searchlight beams as they closed on the enemy. During maneuvers back in the United States, Chennault had brought his P-12 to within 50 feet of a bomber before the crew, blinded by the searchlight, could spot him. The Chinese airmen did almost as well, one of them shooting down three bombers in two nights. Indeed, one night's activity cost the attackers seven of 13 raiders, and operations stopped until the new fighters appeared.

The aircraft hastily dispatched to North China was the Mitsubishi A5M2, a low-wing, single-place monoplane with open cockpit and fixed landing gear. Although its armament was just a pair of 7.9-mm machine guns, the highly maneuverable fighter proved deadly in the hands of skilled pilots. On 18 September 1937, for instance, 27 of these planes, fitted with 35-gallon auxiliary fuel tanks, escorted nine bombers to Nanking and shot down 11 of the 16 Chinese Hawks that tried to intercept.

With better pilots and better planes, the enemy rapidly gained control of the skies over North China. By the end of October, Chennault later admitted, the Chinese Air Force had come to the end of its rope. Chiang's ground forces also were falling back, and the unity of the previous summer was breaking down.

At this point, Russian self-interest again dictated that the Soviet Union come to Chiang's aid, taking the place of the Italians, who had forfeited their influence when they advised that China yield to the Japanese. To counter mounting Japanese pressure along the border between Russia and Manchukuo, Joseph Stalin, the Soviet dictator, began sending airmen and planes to China. The first of more than 300 aircraft and 500 men arrived during October 1937. The machines were among the best in the Red Air Force—twin-engine SB-2 monoplane bombers, I-15 and I-16 fighters. The men deployed in organized squadrons and remained subject to military discipline throughout their tours of duty.

Both fighters, designed by the eminent Nikolai Polikarpov, were stubby single-seaters powered by radial engines. The older, more maneuverable I-15bis was a biplane with a fixed landing gear, while the I-16 monoplane had a retractable landing gear and a top speed of about 280 miles per hour, some 50 miles per hour faster than the other aircraft. Chennault found both fighters impressive; he especially liked their rugged construction and firepower—four machine guns compared with two in the

Crew at work in a plant built for aircraft repair

Japanese A5M. He once saw a Russian pilot, pursued by a Mitsubishi, execute a snap roll during a steep dive, a maneuver that he described as incredible. He knew of no other airplane that could have held together during so violent a maneuver.

The Soviet fighter contingent—Red Air Force units flying their own aircraft—figured in one of the great aerial victories of 1938. Sure that the Japanese would celebrate Emperor Hirohito's birthday, 29 April, with an air attack of some kind, Chennault worked with Mow and the Russian commanders to set a trap for the enemy. On the 28th they ordered aloft all the fighters based at Hankow, a large city on the Yangtze River, making sure that local Japanese agents saw them depart. Late in the day, hugging the treetops, Hankow's aerial defenders returned to bases in the region.

The enemy took the bait, early the following morning sending out bombers escorted by fighters. Despite having auxiliary fuel tanks, the escort was low on gasoline by the time the strike force approached the city. Alerted by a warning net, Soviet and Chinese aircraft were waiting. Some 20 Chinese pilots flying Russian planes made the initial interception, harassing the formation and forcing the escort to burn additional fuel. A few minutes away, 40 Soviet pilots bided their time, waiting their turn to pounce. When they finally struck, the A5Ms barely had fuel enough to defend themselves, let alone protect the bombers. The defensive force claimed the destruction of 36 of the 39 Japanese aircraft, an estimate that probably was not far from the mark, while losing 11 fighters.

The Russians, with Chennault's help in planning, also made the most daring bombing raid of the year—a sudden thrust at Taipei, Formosa, by 28 SB-2 bombers. Since the Japanese had neither radar nor organized ground observers, the Russians achieved complete surprise, dropping their bombs and escaping without encountering fighter opposition.

Mow's airmen were eager to outdo the Russians and bomb Japan itself, but none of their bombers could carry a load of high explosive that far. By way of compromise between wish and reality, the Chinese sent a flight of Martin 139s to drop propaganda leaflets on Nagasaki, a city that would be devastated in 1945 by the second atomic bomb. The swift Martins encountered no opposition, but one plane nearly crashed because the crew scattered the leaflets from the cockpit instead of dropping them from the bomb bay. A bundle became lodged against the bomber's control column, forcing the nose down, but the pilot kicked the leaflets aside and pulled out of the dive.

In spite of these successes, the Japanese gradually gained control of North China, capturing Nanking and Hankow, forced Chiang to move his capital far inland to Chungking, and seized the port of Canton to the south. The sustained aerial fighting all but wiped out the Chinese Air Force that Chennault had rebuilt since the autumn of 1937. Because time was needed to train replacements and obtain new equipment, Mme. Chiang resurrected an idea first suggested when the Japanese invaded Manchuria seven years earlier—the hiring of foreign aviators not to serve as instructors but actually to fight for China.

Ironically, in the light of his later recruitment of the Flying Tigers, Chennault opposed the plan. He argued that the scheme would attract more adventurers than disciplined pilots. Hence the projected International Squadron would probably have died aborning, if a businessman named William Pawley, who was selling American-built planes, had not offered Chiang some two dozen Vultee V-11s. These single-engine monoplanes had a range of 2,000 miles, enough to permit strikes on coastal shipping. In order to get them into action as quickly as possible, Chennault agreed to the recruiting of foreigners. Soon a mixed group of Americans and Europeans was on board.

Some good men signed up to fight for China, among them Jim Allison, who had flown against German and Italian aviators during the Spanish Civil War, but the average hired hand, in Chennault's words, "subsisted almost entirely on high-octane beverages." Although the International Squadron did fly some successful strikes, the members tended to spend too much time drinking and talking. Indeed, their contempt for security soon put them out of business. On the afternoon before a planned mission against Tsinan in North China, the unit's Vultees were loaded with bombs and fuel for an early morning takeoff. Many of the volunteers then retired to their favorite bars, where they boasted about the coming attack. Japanese agents overheard them, enemy bombers appeared overhead even before the sun had set, and by dark every aircraft assigned to the volunteers had been destroyed.

During 1938 and 1939, fighting erupted between Russia and Japan. The Red Air Force not only met this threat, dispatching formations numbering hundreds of planes against the Japanese, but also kept supplying Chiang with modern aircraft, though it could not maintain its combat squadrons in China. Chennault, meanwhile, purchased American-built trainers and set up a flight school at Kunming in Yunnan province, where his staff taught Chinese to fly the Russian I-15s and I-16s. To protect Kunming and other targets nearby, he set about building fighter dispersal strips and creating the warning net, linked by radio and telephone to a central headquarters, that would later serve the Flying Tigers so well.

But Japanese strength proved overwhelming. A single raid on Chungking, Chiang's provisional capital, killed more than 10,000 people. Flames started by incendiary bombs consumed row after row of flimsy wooden shacks. In desperation, Chennault mounted two Madsen 23-mm cannon beneath the wings of a Curtiss Hawk 75A, creating the kind of cannon-equipped fighter that he had advocated while at the Air Corps Tactical School. This hybrid was an instant success. George Weigle, one of the

Japan's most famous aircraft—the A6M Zero (captured by the Chinese)

most capable veterans of the disbanded International Squadron, shot down four bombers with the Madsen guns before he was killed in a crash that destroyed the modified Curtiss.

Despite Weigle's efforts and the influx of war material from the Soviet Union, Japan retained control of the skies. This domination resulted in part from the introduction of another new fighter. This aircraft was the Mitsubishi A6M—the famous Zero, so called because the Imperial Japanese Navy had designated it the Model 0 carrier fighter. This maneuverable and hard-hitting newcomer outfought both the Russian I-16s and the recently purchased Hawk 75As.

In October 1940, with Japanese troops firmly in control of China's major seaports and hostile aircraft attacking at will, Chiang summoned Chennault to the capital. World War II was on, and the Soviet Union, Germany and Great Britain were concentrating their resources in Europe; France had already been defeated. The likeliest source of aircraft for China therefore seemed to be the United States. Would Chennault lead a mission to the United States to buy modern fighter planes and hire trained American pilots to fly them? If he was successful, the men and machines he acquired would hold off the Japanese until a Chinese Air Force, trained and equipped, could take over.

This was now Chennault's vision, too. Of course he would go.

# 4. Seeking American Help

As he prepared to depart for the United States, Chennault weighed the possibility of organizing the kind of volunteer force that Chiang wanted. Perhaps he really could succeed. After all, the most reliable members of the International Squadron—men like George Weigle and Jim Allison— had been Americans, and a number of military and naval aviators were leaving the country to fight for Canada or Great Britain. He might be able to persuade some of these young idealists to serve in China.

He hoped this trip would prove more successful than his last visit to the United States. He had spent Christmas 1939 with his family in Louisiana and had used the occasion to renew his request to return to active duty with the Army Air Corps. That service, however, wanted no part of a cantankerous, overage fighter pilot grown almost deaf from the roar of airplane engines. Understandably, he refused to accept the official explanation that no funds were available to recall officers from retirement, though this could possibly have been the case.

Chennault was torn between loyalty toward his country and admiration for his employer. His realization that war would inevitably break out between Japan and the United States spurred him onward in his futile effort to return to active duty. Yet he also wanted to finish the job Chiang had given him.

Flying Tiger P-40 comes in for a landing at Kunming, China

Unlike many westerners, Chennault had not become disillusioned by the corruption so deeply rooted in Chinese life. Everyone from shopkeeper to field marshal seemed to expect a bribe of some sort, and Chiang had even provided Chennault with a special account for this purpose. The American, however, refused to draw upon this fund, substituting fountain pens or mechanical pencils for more expensive gifts and still managing to delight the Chinese who appeared to like gadgets of every sort. In brief, he saw no reason to reform Chinese life. Instead he concentrated on keeping himself from being corrupted.

As for Chiang, Chennault marveled at the Generalissimo's skill in extracting sound ideas from advisers of dubious honesty or loyalty. Somehow the Chinese leader played off one man's weakness against another's strength, holding together the intricate and fragile web of alliances. Time and again, Japan seemed on the verge of triumph, but Chiang managed to survive. Perhaps the recruiting of a few squadrons of American planes and pilots might tip the balance; Chennault intended to try.

When he arrived in Washington, Chennault did something uncharacteristic: he tried to compromise. He attempted to return to active duty with the Air Corps while at the same time working to revive the declining fortunes of the Chinese Air Force. His earlier requests for an opportunity to teach Army pilots what he had learned in China about Japanese tactics had resulted in the offer of a nonflying assignment as an instructor at the

Coast Artillery School, Fortress Monroe, Va. Once again he received the offer, sweetened this time with the promise of promotion from captain to major, and again he refused, since lecturing to antiaircraft officers had little to do with fighter tactics. To the Air Corps hierarchy, Chennault remained just another retired captain seeking a steady job. "I never did convince them," he sorrowfully admitted, "that I was not just looking for a regular pay check but really wanted to do a specific job that I knew was being badly neglected."

Rejected by the Air Corps, he now concentrated on the mission Chiang had assigned him. In this task he worked with the Nationalist representative in the United States, T. V. Soong, Chiang's brother-in-law and a man not unlike Chennault in temperament and dedication. The Chinese diplomat was as competent in matters of finance as Chennault was in aviation, and the two could be equally impatient with authority. Soong had raised the money that had paid Chiang's armies during the late 1920s, but his bluntness and contempt for traditional protocol had driven the Generalissimo to distraction. Chennault compared Soong to an eccentric relief pitcher, banished to the bullpen only to be called upon whenever the team was in trouble. The Nationalist cause was in deep trouble as the year 1941 began, and Soong would have to call upon all his skills in helping save it.

One of Soong's strong points was his relationship with the American

Cargo plane and fighter: Curtiss C-46 Commando and P-40

press. He introduced Chennault to a pair of influential journalists, Edgar Ansel Mowrer and Joseph Alsop, who were startled to hear of the dominance of the Zero fighter. Obviously, Soong's original plan to buy up obsolescent American planes like the Curtiss P-36 or the Navy's Brewster F2A-1 Buffalo would merely provide fodder for the 20-mm cannon carried by the Mitsubishi. The two newspapermen doubted that the United States government would divert first-line fighters from its own armed forces or from production allotted to Great Britain to assist China.

Within the government, however, pro-China sentiment had been growing. The deliberate bombing of the gunboat USS *Panay* in 1937 had offered convincing evidence of Japan's increasing contempt for the western democracies. Moreover, President Franklin D. Roosevelt had an abiding interest in China, where his family had traded during the mid-19th century, and he sensed that Japanese ambitions extended far beyond the subjugation of China. Much of the President's information on China came from a former commander of the Marine guard at the Little White House in Warm Springs, Ga. This officer, Captain Evans F. Carlson, now served as an attaché in China, where he traveled widely, relaying back home stories of heroism and self-sacrifice but remaining insensitive to the darker currents of Chinese politics. Reports like those from Carlson outweighed the gloomier assessments from observers such as Colonel Stilwell, the military attaché, and helped create an idealized view of China that gained acceptance throughout the administration.

But this attitude did not help Soong when he conferred with Secretary of the Treasury Henry Morgenthau about borrowing money to buy 500 planes and other military equipment. Although Morgenthau, too, wanted to help the Chinese, he had to advise the prospective buyer that trying to obtain 500 planes was like asking for 500 stars. The American aviation industry was straining to supply the British while at the same time providing modern aircraft to the U.S. Army, Navy and Marine Corps; bombers and fighters simply could not be spared. Luckily for Soong, the British purchasing mission agreed to let China acquire a hundred Curtiss P-40B Tomahawks destined for the Royal Air Force, provided that a newer fighter would later be available to replace them.

Shortages of aircraft and of trained American crews doomed a hastily sketched plan, inspired by Chiang and presented by Soong and his Chinese colleagues. They outlined for President Roosevelt an ambitious scheme to sign up volunteers who would fly B-17s with Chinese markings against the cities of Japan, dropping bombs where General Mow's handful of Martin 139s had scattered leaflets. Secretary Morgenthau and Secretary of State Cordell Hull endorsed the idea, but General George C. Marshall, Army Chief of Staff, vetoed it. He could not allow an expanding Air Corps to break up its few trained and equipped Flying Fortress squadrons to place men and aircraft under foreign control halfway around the world.

In purchasing the hundred Tomahawks, to be paid for out of $25 million credited by the U.S. government to Chinese accounts, Soong enlisted the aid of William Pawley, who had sold Chiang the Vultee V-11s flown by the ill-fated International Squadron, and his brother Edwin. Together they organized the Central Aircraft Manufacturing Company, which would hire 350 pilots and mechanics, pay their salaries and expenses, and act as agents in buying the P-40s. At the time, Chennault and the Pawleys worked together smoothly, William declaring that the ex-captain was "indisputably among the informed few who know just about all there is to know concerning aerial warfare against the Jap." For a time, the brothers would share the danger of Japanese bombs with Chennault's volunteers based in Burma. By the end of the war, however, Chennault had broken with the two men, and in his memoirs he fired a three-page broadside at William, though Chennault's anger may have stemmed from his own impatience with circumstances rather than from any misconduct by the brothers.

Complementing the work of the Central Aircraft Manufacturing Company was China Defense Supplies, Inc. President Roosevelt was so interested in aiding China that he appointed Thomas G. Corcoran, one of his closest assistants, as general counsel of China Defense Supplies. Tommy the Cork, as the President had nicknamed him, proved a fortunate choice, for despite an unsuccessful first meeting, during which he dismissed Chennault as a fanatic, the Washington lawyer developed a deep respect for the flier. "Chennault was a born teacher," Corcoran recalled; "he explained enough in an hour to make me believe I was dealing with something original, whether it was genius or madness." Corcoran decided in favor of genius, though in reporting the conversation to President Roosevelt he conceded that he would hate to be Chennault's boss, for he realized that the airman's talents could not be contained within a box on someone's organizational chart. Chennault might play Drake to Roosevelt's Queen Elizabeth I, but he definitely needed a strong leader, whom he respected, and a free hand in carrying out that leader's grand design.

While Central Aircraft Manufacturing and China Defense Supplies were getting under way, the President sought some means to circumvent the laws designed to ensure American neutrality, so that Great Britain and China could receive direct aid. Roosevelt got his way when Congress passed the Lend-Lease Act, signed into law in March 1941, which enabled the United States to lend or lease war material to nations whose defense seemed essential to American security. Armed with this authority, the President cast about for the kinds of equipment that China needed, only to discover that Chiang had never prepared a systematic request for assistance. All that was available was Chennault's plan to buy new pursuit planes and the Soong proposal to acquire obsolete aircraft and other surplus equipment.

At Chiang's invitation, Roosevelt sent one of his aides, Lauchlin Currie, to help the Chinese prepare a lend-lease shopping list. When he arrived in China, Currie discovered an armed truce between Nationalists and Communists. Chiang's hatred of the Communists was "very deep," the Presidential emissary reported, "and his distrust of them is complete." This loathing, he told the President, did not stem "from the usual antagonism between 'property interests' and 'the proletariat,' " but resulted from the Generalissimo's lifetime determination to unify China and the fact that "the Communists have been the only group he has not been able to buy off, liquidate, or suppress."

Despite this deeply rooted enmity between Chiang and the Communists, Currie remained confident that "hostilities on a large scale" would not erupt between the two factions "in the near future." The Nationalist leader, after all, wished to assure the President "that he had the situation well in hand, that he knew exactly how far he could go, and that there would be no civil war." Chou En-lai, Mao Tse-tung's chief adviser, had seemed "equally desirous of avoiding a showdown at this time." Currie emphasized, however, that the conflict between Nationalists and Communists was being postponed, rather than resolved. "There is," he told Roosevelt, "a very dubious prospect of maintaining political stability in the postwar period."

While visiting the air base at Chengtu, Currie discovered a handful of Russians drinking at the club. These men, he learned, were the advance party for a 300-man contingent expected in a matter of weeks. Parked at the airfield were some 50 pursuits and 50 bombers, fresh from factories in the Soviet Union, and another 200 planes were on order. Besides SB-2s and I-16s, the Chinese had negotiated for newer aircraft, fighters with top speeds in excess of 330 miles per hour. This Soviet assistance, the prospect of lend-lease aid, and the volunteer group being organized by Chennault together seemed to assure the revival of China's air force.

Scarcely had Currie visited Chengtu and inspected one of the recently arrived SB-2s than Joseph Stalin dealt the Nationalist cause a severe jolt. On 13 April 1941 he entered into a nonaggression pact with Japan. Thus, having neutralized the threat from Manchukuo by means of diplomacy, the Soviet dictator no longer needed to divert men and aircraft to China.

Currie, who had returned to the United States when the Russo-Japanese agreement was announced, immediately began making the rounds of aircraft manufacturers, arranging to obtain planes that would make up for the canceled Soviet aid. From the Republic and Vultee companies he ordered almost 250 second-line fighters, while Douglas offered a few B-23s, a twin-engine bomber based on the DC-3 transport, and Lockheed released some Hudson bombers that the British could not use. If all

Republic P-43s of the Chinese Air Force

went well, China would still manage to have the nucleus of an air force besides Chennault's volunteers.

Meanwhile, until combat-ready Chinese pilots took to the air in the Republic P-43s and Vultee P-48s that Currie had found, the defense of China would rest in the hands of American volunteers flying an airplane their leader disliked. Chennault objected to the Tomahawk's lack of an optical gunsight and the absence of fittings for bomb racks and auxiliary fuel tanks. He also complained about the substitution of six British .303-caliber machine guns for the two .50-caliber and four .30-caliber weapons carried by Air Corps models, a change that seemed likely to complicate the problem of obtaining ammunition. But the plane's gravest disability, he believed, was its 1,150-horsepower Allison liquid-cooled engine.

For Curtiss, the manufacturer, and for the Army Air Corps, however, this power plant was the principal attraction of the P-40B. Back in 1937 Donovan Berlin, chief designer for the Curtiss organization, realized that he had wrung all the performance possible from the P-36, a design he had completed three years before. The Air Corps, influenced by new European fighters, had become fascinated with the liquid-cooled engine, which offered a much smaller frontal area than the radial and lent itself to streamlining that reduced drag and increased speed. Working for one of the more conservative of American plane builders, Berlin came up with a low-risk suggestion. Why not mate the proven P-36 design with the new Allison engine to produce a fighter with a top speed of 370 miles per hour?

Berlin's airplane, originally called the Hawk 81, never achieved this goal, but it came close enough to win acceptance by the Air Corps, which designated it the P-40, by the French and by the British. The P-40Bs that Chennault inherited had a top speed of about 350 miles per hour at 15,000 feet, but the lack of a supercharger limited the service ceiling to only 32,000 feet. The Tomahawk, in short, was not a fast, highly maneuverable interceptor; instead, Berlin's design was a compromise, reflecting uncertainty within the Air Corps whether to invest in a rugged, low-flying fighter-bomber or a fast high-altitude interceptor like the British Spitfire. Given the prevailing confidence that the bomber would always get through, fighter-bomber characteristics prevailed.

Yet, in the hands of a skilled pilot, the P-40B was a deadly fighting machine. John Alison, an Air Corps second lieutenant, proved this when he conducted a demonstration flight for Mow and the other members of the Chinese purchasing mission. Climbing into a Tomahawk fresh from the Curtiss factory at Buffalo, N.Y., he took off from Bolling Field, Washington, D.C., and in five minutes got more speed, climb and maneuverability out of Berlin's design than Chennault had believed possible. No sooner had the young officer landed than the Chinese surrounded Chennault, lavishing praise on the Tomahawk. We need a hundred of these planes, they told him. No, Chennault replied, what you need is a hundred Johnny Alisons.

John Alison—the kind of skilled pilot sought by the Flying Tigers

The veteran airman was right. Difficult though it was, obtaining fighter planes had been the easier part of the job. Now he faced the truly formidable challenge of working with the Pawleys to recruit a hundred pilots with Alison's skill, plus the staff officers, mechanics and other specialists who would support them in combat.

# 5. Ruffians, Renegades and Idealists

Almost 20 years after the war, Thomas Corcoran addressed a meeting of Flying Tiger veterans in Los Angeles. He recalled how an A. E. Housman poem, "Epitaph for an Army of Mercenaries," had inspired Franklin Roosevelt to help Chennault recruit his volunteers. The poem told of a band of men who, "in the days when Heaven was falling," defended what God had abandoned and "saved the sum of things for pay." The President saw the men of the American Volunteer Group as mercenaries in an idealistic cause and on 15 April 1941, with a minimum of publicity, issued an executive order permitting officers in the Air Corps, naval aviation and Marine Corps aviation to resign, sign contracts with Central Aircraft Manufacturing and fly for Chennault.

Without the President's intervention, the Flying Tigers might never have taken to the air. Hap Arnold, whose report of the 1934 West Coast maneuvers had come under attack by Chennault, now commanded the Army Air Corps. Accompanied by Lauchlin Currie, the retired captain called upon General Arnold and asked his cooperation in forming a volunteer group. Arnold flatly refused, declaring that he could not jeopardize Air Corps expansion by allowing either staff officers or trained pilots to resign and serve in China. Admiral John Towers, in charge of naval aviation,

Flying Tigers John Alison (l.), David Hill, Albert Baumler, Mack Mitchell as members of the 23d Fighter Group

proved equally uncooperative, and for the same reasons, until the President issued his directive.

In the wake of this order, Secretary of the Navy Frank Knox and Secretary of War Henry L. Stimson issued instructions permitting recruiters from the Central Aircraft Manufacturing Company to contact eligible Navy, Marine Corps and Army aviators. As nearly as Chennault could tell, Secretary Knox cooperated fully, harboring no grievance against those who volunteered (and, later, welcoming them back when their tours had ended). In Chennault's opinion, Arnold was less cooperative, however, refusing to release staff officers—who admittedly were in short supply—and apparently showing resentment toward fliers who cast their lot with the Flying Tigers.

Once Knox and Stimson had granted access to service installations, recruiters began making their rounds. In charge of the effort was Richard Aldworth, a former Air Corps pilot, who suffered from a kidney ailment that eventually killed him. Setting up an office in his room at Walter Reed Hospital in Washington, D.C., he coordinated the efforts of a half-dozen men, including C. B. Adair and Harry Claiborne—both Army-trained pilots—and Rutledge Irvine, a retired naval aviator. These recruiters visited bases from Bolling Field to San Diego, by way of Quantico, Va., and Pensacola, Fla.

At each stop, Irvine or one of the others offered eligible pilots and

**40**

technicians a one-year contract with Central Aircraft Manufacturing at a salary varying from $250 to $750 a month, plus allowances for rations, travel and the like. The agreement made no mention of combat, merely stating that the individual would "manufacture, repair and operate aircraft." Although the contract did not spell it out, recruiters assured prospective volunteers they would receive a $500 bonus for every confirmed aerial victory. The Chinese government not only honored this obligation but eventually agreed to pay the same amount for the confirmed destruction of Japanese planes on the ground.

Unlike the Soviet airmen who had fought in China a few years earlier, the American volunteers were not subject to military discipline. Their relationship to the group commander was that of employee to boss. Chennault could, for example, levy fines for minor offenses or fire any volunteer who proved insubordinate, was a drunk or drug addict or revealed military information. Within the limitations on his authority, Chennault was determined to prevent his organization from suffering the fate of the old International Squadron.

The 240 pilots and supporting technicians who signed up did so for a variety of reasons. "The true story of the Flying Tigers in China," said Tom Trumble, a Nebraskan who served as Chennault's secretary, "is the aggregate of the separate stories of the nearly 300 men. Nearly all were youngsters who for the love of adventure or hope of gain took the gamble and volunteered to serve under an unknown leader and fight for an unknown government."

As Trumble indicated, a variety of motives had prompted the volunteers, both those who signed up in the United States and the 50 or so recruited in the Orient. Some of them were genuine soldiers of fortune, like Albert J. ("Ajax") Baumler, who had fought for the Loyalists in Spain. Passed over by the Air Corps, which considered him too undisciplined to become a successful fighter pilot, Baumler had scored aerial victories in the Russian-built I-15 biplane and I-16 monoplane.

His first mission for the Loyalists, flown in an I-15, had ended in frustration, when his intended victim, an Italian CR-32 biplane, escaped unharmed and Baumler limped back to his base with engine trouble. But his luck promptly changed as in quick succession he helped down one Fiat, single-handedly destroyed another of the Italian-built fighters and a German Heinkel He 51, and possibly shot down a second Heinkel. After switching to the faster I-16, he scored a confirmed victory over a CR-32 and possibly destroyed another plane of this type.

One of the last men to join the American Volunteer Group, Baumler was headed for China when the Japanese attacked Pearl Harbor. The crew of the Boeing Clipper on which he had booked passage learned of the bombing on reaching Wake Island, had the plane refueled and turned back. Unable to honor his contract with the American Volunteer Group, Baumler returned to active duty with the Army Air Forces and eventually served in China under Chennault.

Some of the volunteers were sons of missionary parents who had labored in the Far East. Among these was Jim Howard, who would participate in the Flying Tigers' first combat action. Howard and the others like him seemed to combine idealism with a genuine affection for the Chinese people.

In addition, there were the skilled fliers thoroughly at home in the sky but ill suited to military life. This category included First Lieutenant Gregory Boyington, USMC, who in six years of active duty had plunged so deeply in debt that each month he had to submit a report to Marine Corps headquarters detailing how he was paying off his numerous creditors. When a retired Air Corps captain, probably either Adair or Claiborne, arrived at the Pensacola Naval Air Station, where Boyington served as a flight instructor, he did not contact the 28-year-old marine. Aware that he almost certainly would not receive promotion to captain and would have to leave the corps, Boyington took the initiative, searched out the recruiter and tried to talk his way onto the Central Aircraft Manufacturing payroll. This decision was his first tentative step toward becoming "Pappy" Boyington, the World War II legend.

At first, Chennault's representative seemed reluctant to accept Boyington, claiming that combat veterans were standing in line to sign up, but he soon acknowledged that room might somehow be found for an experienced instructor. Besides, he assured Boyington, Japanese pilots not only flew second-rate airplanes but also wore thick eyeglasses, so wartime experience might not be essential. The marine suspected that very few war veterans were trying to join the group and that Japanese aviators and planes might prove more formidable than the recruiter cared to admit, but he was not about to challenge the story. After all, Boyington had to tell a few lies of his own if he was to pass himself off as a self-disciplined and sober individual who was gallantly sacrificing a bright future to fight for China's survival. He obviously succeeded—he signed a $675-per-month contract as a flight leader.

Still other volunteers were outright idealists, like Curtis Smith, a 35-year-old Marine Corps reservist who had recently completed refresher training at Pensacola. Although a qualified pilot, he was going along as an adjutant, filling an assignment for which Chennault had hoped to find a more experienced Air Corps staff officer. During the voyage to the Orient, Boyington had long conversations with Smith and discovered that the Georgia-born volunteer had joined the group to fight for democracy and that he was willing to die for that principle.

Among the nonflying members of the American Volunteer Group was Joseph Alsop, the journalist who had confidently declared that the United States would never provide modern fighters for the defense of China. Now Chennault had 100 P-40Bs originally destined for Great Britain and trained pilots that the American armed forces could certainly use. Alsop was so delighted to be proved wrong that he offered to serve on the staff of the man who had done the impossible.

Despite the recruiters' glib talk of enlisting combat veterans of the fighting in China or Spain, the experience logged by the volunteer fliers proved as varied as their reasons for joining. Of the hundred pilots, only Baumler had actually shot down a hostile airplane, and about half of them had never sat in the cockpit of a fighter. George Burgard and Charley Bond, for instance, had flown Army bombers; Bob Neale and David ("Tex") Hill, naval aviators like most of the volunteers, were dive-bomber pilots. Henry Gilbert, far from being a combat veteran, had recently won his Army wings; he was just 21 years old. But one of the Navy airmen, Louis Hoffman, had logged almost as much fighter time as Chennault. He was, in fact, only eight years younger than the group commander.

The State Department cooperated enthusiastically in President Roosevelt's plan to aid China. Chennault's volunteers had no problem obtaining passports that described them as clerks, students, even bankers—anything but what they really were. Several men, Boyington among them, traveled in the guise of missionaries. Chennault's passport described him as a Louisiana farmer.

Early in July 1941 Chennault took the Pan American Clipper across the

David ("Tex") Hill became a key member of the Tigers

Pacific, pausing en route to confer with various officers of the Army Air Forces, as the Air Corps had recently been redesignated. Among them was Howard Davidson, who commanded Chennault's old squadron in Hawaii, a unit now equipped with P-40s. In the Philippines he talked with Generals Harold George and Henry Clagett. According to Chennault's account, George promptly requested permission to join the American Volunteer Group, only to be turned down by the War Department. Clagett later would undertake a mission to China to study the needs of the Chinese Air Force.

Except for Baumler, who got no farther than Wake Island, the rest of the group went to the Orient by ship, traveling in sections of 25 or 30, with one of the volunteers in charge. These leaders, however, could persuade but not command, and keeping the men from gorging themselves on food or drinking themselves senseless proved almost impossible. Some of the section leaders organized calisthenics for their men, combining threats with personal example to get the men to burn off the fat they were putting on.

The fliers responded with cursing, threats and practical jokes, some of which were more brutal than funny. In his book *Baa Baa Black Sheep*, Boyington relates how two members of his section faked a brawl, while another man ran to summon the leader. Curtis Smith, the person in charge, burst onto the scene and grabbed the supposed combatants, one with each hand. While he was thus occupied, another member of the section flattened him with a punch to the eye.

The marathon card games caused several genuine fights, as many a future combat pilot lost bonus money for aerial victories he had not yet won. Although the ships' doctors were kept busy treating cuts and bruises, there were no serious injuries or abiding grudges. The aviators, after all, remained confident they would be wallowing in cash when myopic Japanese began falling before their guns. An uneasiness began to surface, however, when a fellow passenger of Boyington, a transport pilot headed for the Netherlands East Indies, reported that he had never met a Japanese airman who wore glasses.

These antics soon dispelled the myth that these Americans were students, missionaries or whatever their passports claimed. Shortly after sailing, Boyington found himself seated at dinner with fellow passengers who were genuine missionaries. He assumed, however, that they were as phony as he and began regaling them with stories of drunken parties that had preceded his departure from San Francisco. The conversation served only to inspire a sermon, which was preached a few days later, on the evils of being a mercenary.

The various contingents of volunteers caroused their way across the Pacific, stopping at places like Batavia and Surabaya in Java, the island of Bali and Singapore. Almost every stop became the scene of parties that rivaled the San Francisco farewells. Finally, in September 1941, the first members of the American Volunteer Group arrived at Rangoon, Burma, and preparations for combat began.

As the ships of the Dutch-owned Java-Pacific Line were bringing the volunteers to Rangoon, Chennault was making arrangements to set up a training base in British-ruled Burma. Delays in recruiting the volunteers and shipping the P-40s had forced him to abandon his original plan to train at Kunming, for the monsoon rains would be falling by the time the men and planes arrived. Although the British government readily agreed that Central Aircraft Manufacturing could assemble and test the Tomahawks in Burma, the threat from Japanese forces in Indochina dissuaded London from permitting combat training in the colony.

The Pawley brothers and General Mow joined Chennault in pleading with the British to change the decision. The senior air officer, Group Captain E. R. Manning, objected to having a ragtag collection of renegade airmen raising hell in his domain, but the governor and his military commander proved sympathetic to the presence of the volunteers. Mow and his colleagues argued that since neither Japan nor the United States recognized that a state of war existed in China, the members of the American Volunteer Group could not be considered belligerents and could therefore train in Burma without compromising British neutrality toward the Japanese. Gradually Great Britain's officialdom accepted this view, first leasing the Kyedaw airfield near Toungoo to the Chinese government, then permitting strafing practice in the area and finally agreeing to full-scale combat training, provided that Chennault did not use bases in Burma to mount combat operations.

During these hectic negotiations, while Chennault shuttled back and forth among Rangoon, Singapore and Chungking, his only staff officer was Boatner Carney, an old China hand who had worked with him since 1938. Since General Arnold insisted upon holding onto his cadre of experienced staff officers, Chennault began recruiting a staff from among his acquaintances in the Far East. He chose as his executive officer, for example, Harvey Greenlaw, whose wife Olga volunteered to be group statistician and maintain the unit's war diary. She was one of three women in the organization; the other two, Emma Jane Foster and Josephine Stewart, were nurses who assisted the three surgeons recruited by Chennault.

When Gregory Boyington at last arrived in Burma, he was startled by the size of the headquarters Chennault had assembled. In fact, the group commander himself apologized for the number of paper shufflers he employed, explaining that Army policy had prevented him from assembling a staff in the United States. Boyington took him at his word. With the aviator's contempt for the nonflier, the former marine declared that Chennault needed this vast collection of scribes and clerks because it took 10 of them to do one man's work.

In spite of his loathing for many of the staff members, Boyington

The famed Gregory ("Pappy") Boyington (here as a Marine flier)

respected and admired Chennault. He enjoyed the little tricks the older man played, especially the way he always heard what he wasn't supposed to hear, despite the fact that the Air Corps had retired him for deafness. In short, even though he had wrapped himself in a mantle of cynicism, Boyington responded enthusiastically to Chennault's informal approach to military leadership. In his book, Boyington recalled the softball games at Toungoo, in which Chennault always played, swinging furiously, seldom hitting the ball beyond the infield, but running out every dribbler as though a World Series victory depended upon his reaching first base.

Even as the volunteers were embarking from San Francisco and Chennault was beginning the tortuous negotiations for a base in Burma, the P-40 Tomahawks were being shipped to the Orient. In charge of uncrating and assembling the airplanes was Walter Pentecost. While employed by North American Aviation, he had spent nine months at the Allison engine factory in Indianapolis, where he had learned all the intricacies of building and overhauling this liquid-cooled powerplant. His answering a newspaper advertisement for "aviation people" willing to work overseas brought him into contact with the Pawley brothers, who tried to impress prospective mechanics with a slide show that featured views of Burmese pagodas, quaint villages and water buffalo. In Pentecost's case, the sales pitch was unnecessary. "I'd already made up my mind to go," he told a team of interviewers several years later. "I didn't care what they showed me. It was something different, and I was ready." He signed a contract calling for a small salary plus $100 a month for expenses, used as much of it as he could to finance a series of poker games and put aside a sizable amount during the year he worked for the Pawleys.

In May 1941 Pentecost disembarked from the steamer *Karda* at Rangoon, where supplies destined for China normally were unloaded for further shipment overland. Chennault paid a visit and quickly expressed boundless confidence in him. After looking over his makeshift assembly line at Rangoon's Mingaladon airfield, Pentecost was not so sure his skills would prevail. He had only hand tools, plus a crude **A** frame that would support a P-40 fuselage while Burmese laborers bolted the wings in place. With the rainy season fast approaching, his first task was to build a shelter for assembling the fighters. He found the brick shell of a former warehouse, told his workers to roof the structure with bamboo, and then had them pave an adjacent courtyard with brick to serve as a parking site for the finished planes.

The resulting delay, although unavoidable, upset the impatient Chennault, who found the planes still in their crates when he returned to Rangoon in July. He therefore prodded the Pawley brothers into sending several Chinese and American mechanics from their Central Aircraft Manufacturing plant at Loi-Wing, China. Completion of a sheltered assembly area, together with the arrival of the experienced technicians, then enabled

P-40s are rebuilt in this Chinese factory

Pentecost to make rapid progress. His crew completed 22 P-40s in August, 21 in September, 29 in October and the remaining 27 in November. One of the original 100 had been lost overboard en route to the Orient.

After brief test flights, the planes were flown by the volunteers from Mingaladon to Kyedaw airdrome at Toungoo, where other mechanics and armorers installed radios, oxygen equipment, guns and crude ring-and-post gunsights. Chennault's trio of surgeons—Doctors Tom Gentry, Lewis Richards and Sam Prevo—looked after the health of the men, helping them to become acclimatized to the rain and oppressive heat. By the time the planes were fitted out, enough healthy fliers were available to begin training in earnest.

# 6. In Training at Toungoo

Kyedaw airfield at Toungoo boasted a 4,000-foot asphalt runway that permitted operations to continue during the rainy season. Planes could take off and land here, while aircraft based at Kunming remained mired by the thundershowers that soaked the grass runways and parking areas. To provide shelter from the monsoons, Kyedaw had new barracks built of teakwood and roofed with straw. The facilities at this base were a considerable improvement over the converted warehouse at Rangoon.

Although Kyedaw afforded these advantages, the difference between urban Rangoon and the hamlet of Toungoo, where Kyedaw was located, dismayed the volunteers. At Rangoon, they had had the Silver Bar as their informal headquarters, and while they waited for Pentecost and his men to assemble the P-40s, they had spent their time drinking and staging water buffalo rodeos in the streets. Soon the local press was printing editorials condemning the American ruffians. As Manning, the British air officer, had warned, the presence of these flying mercenaries was proving a threat to law and order. Rangoon's British upper class breathed easier when the wild Americans moved inland to Toungoo, a collection of bamboo huts surrounded by forest.

Chennault's volunteers loaded their belongings into railroad chair cars and went rattling along the narrow-gauge line linking Rangoon with Toungoo. En route, many of them amused themselves by aiming pistols through the open sliding doors and blasting away at telegraph poles. When they reached their destination, they learned that sunlight on the thatched roof could turn the interior of a wooden barracks into an oven. At dusk, as temperatures dropped, clouds of mosquitoes rose from stagnant pools to feast on American flesh. Scorpions scuttled across barracks floors to hide in boots or clothing; their sting could raise welts the size of golf balls. Only at Kyedaw could a pilot sprawl on his bunk beneath a mosquito net, his back swollen from a scorpion bite, while his barracks mates were beating a cobra to death.

Life in the wilds of Burma proved too much for a handful of the volunteers, who resigned and booked passage back to the United States. The others hung grimly on, playing hundreds of innings of softball, quarreling occasionally and sometimes giving vent to their wrath by firing their pistols at trees. Indeed, a spent bullet fired by a marksman more angry than accurate caused the group's first casualty, nicking John T. Sommers, a former Air Corps sergeant now a clerk in the operations section.

Normal military discipline was impossible with this group of contract aviators, and Chennault wisely avoided the customs and practices that so many of his men had found distasteful during their service careers. "On the ground," he later wrote, "we tried to live as nearly as possible under the circumstances as a normal American community." Weekly group meetings disposed of routine business by majority vote. There was no saluting, unless an individual chose to salute the senior man, and no guard house. "Rigid discipline," said Chennault, "was confined to the air and combat matters." This discipline, enforced by fines or dismissal, began during training session at the airfield near Toungoo.

The basic course taught by Chennault consisted of 72 hours of classroom instruction and 60 hours in the air, though some late arrivals missed a few lectures. A typical day began at 0600 as a number of volunteers gathered before a blackboard in a makeshift classroom while Chennault, using the skills he had first learned in teachers college, held forth on everything from aerobatics to geopolitics. Afterward, the volunteers might climb into their P-40s, first for familiarization and later to practice the tactics their leader had chalked on the blackboard. The evening, despite the swarming insects, was the usual time for athletics.

During his introductory lecture, Chennault outlined the strategic situation in China. With Japan in control of the principal mainland ports and much of the coastline, supplies destined for China had to come either by way of Rangoon, where the group's P-40s had been unloaded, or from a railhead in Russian Turkestan by road through Sinkiang into northwestern China. As a result of the German invasion in June 1941, the Soviets had little matériel to spare, and Burma had become the gateway to China.

**51**

Tigers are high above Asia en route to the target

Except for three months during the late summer and early autumn of 1940, when Great Britain had yielded to Japanese pressure and cut off the flow of supplies, cargo had been deposited at Rangoon, shipped by narrow-gauge railway to Lashio, then loaded on trucks for the arduous journey over the Burma Road to Chungking. A narrow route twisting among towering mountains, the Burma Road was not only China's lifeline but also a source of tremendous profits to those who operated it. In the spring of 1941 an American official estimated that 14,000 tons of cargo had to leave Lashio if 5,000 tons was to reach Chungking; the balance was either stolen or consumed en route. Obviously, supplying a Kunming-based volunteer group would be a formidable task.

After describing China's plight, Chennault analyzed the enemy. Unlike some of his recruiters back in the United States, he acknowledged the ability of Japanese aviators. "They have been drilled for hundreds of hours," he told his men, "in flying precise formations and rehearsing set tactics for each situation they may encounter." The Japanese, in short, always flew by the book, and Chennault had that book—copies of captured manuals—translated into English and issued to the volunteers. The enemy was brave—bomber crews, for instance, tried to maintain their assigned place in a formation even though the other aircraft were being shot down all around them—but in Chennault's opinion he lacked self-reliance and could not adapt to rapidly changing situations. The volunteers should

therefore try to break up the hostile formation, whether fighter or bomber, and force the Japanese to improvise.

The enemy usually would be flying the Zero fighter (the A6M), now beginning to appear at Japanese airfields in Indochina that were within range of Toungoo, and the new Mitsubishi G4M1 twin-engine bomber. Once again Chennault had a mimeographed publication on the subject. Each of his pilots received complete descriptions of these airplanes and other Japanese craft, including diagrams that showed the vulnerable areas such as fuel tanks, oil coolers, oxygen flasks and bomb bays. By way of examination, he took chalk in hand, sketched the outline of a particular type on the blackboard, drew colored circles around the vital spots, and then erased the drawing. He next called upon one of the pilots—Boyington, for example, or Bob Neale, formerly a Navy ensign—to duplicate the drawing. In this way, the men learned not only to identify enemy aircraft but to fire instinctively at a critical area. "My methods," said Chennault, "were simple and direct, with plenty of repetition to make the lessons stick. In a fight you seldom have time to think, and it is training and reflexes that count."

In the hands of a competent pilot, the Mitsubishi Zero fighter was a dangerous weapon. Designed by Jiro Horikoshi in 1939, the year the P-40 appeared, the Japanese plane represented an entirely new design rather than the revision of an old one. The needs of the Imperial Navy, to which Horikoshi submitted his plans, dictated the Zero's strengths and weak-

Chennault and Fourteenth Air Force staff study a map of South China

nesses. Lightweight construction and fittings for an auxiliary gasoline tank ensured the range necessary for long overwater flights, but the need to reduce weight forced the designer to dispense with self-sealing integral fuel cells and armor protection for the pilot. To compensate for the resulting vulnerability, Horikoshi emphasized nimbleness, a quality prized by Japan's naval aviators. "They can turn on a dime," Chennault said of these aircraft, "and climb almost straight up. If they can get you into a turning combat, they are deadly."

Besides being maneuverable, the handsome Zero was heavily armed, mounting two 7.9-mm machine guns synchronized to fire through the propeller arc and a 20-mm cannon in each wing. The cannon, however, had a comparatively low muzzle velocity, reducing accuracy at long range. Horikoshi's aerodynamically clean, low-wing monoplane featured an enclosed cockpit, an innovation that Japanese naval aviators had resisted for years, and a wide-track undercarriage for ease of operation from both carrier decks and unimproved airstrips at advanced bases. The A6M2, Model 21, the standard version in 1941, was powered by a 925-horsepower radial engine that gave it a top speed of 336 miles per hour at 19,000 feet and a service ceiling of about 34,000 feet.

The cigar-shaped Mitsubishi G4M1 bomber shared many of the weaknesses of the Zero fighter. The Imperial Japanese Navy had again emphasized range at the expense of protection. The result was a fast but vulnerable shoulder-wing monoplane. Although well armed in comparison with its contemporaries, the G4M burned easily because of its unprotected fuel tanks.

Against these foes, Chennault expected his pilots to use the strengths of the P-40—firepower and rugged construction that permitted greater diving speed—to exploit enemy weaknesses—lighter construction, lack of armor and easily punctured metal fuel tanks. "Use your speed and diving power," he told them, "to make a pass, shoot and break away." He warned against trying to outmaneuver the Zero or blundering into the cone of fire from Japanese guns, especially the tail "stinger" mounted in the G4M. For mutual protection, and to increase firepower, the volunteers were to attack in two-plane teams. Allowing for the improvements in aircraft, these tactics were essentially the same as those he had advocated during his Air Corps days.

Nor did Chennault neglect the importance of early warning, something he had always emphasized. He carefully explained how the outposts around Chungking and Kunming could enable a control center to guide the P-40s into position to intercept the enemy. He even tried to persuade Group Captain Manning to let him set up a network of observers to help protect Kyedaw. The Australian-born officer refused, however, choosing to rely on radar sets located to defend Rangoon and Moulmein, but useless in the Toungoo region.

Lectures on subjects like enemy aircraft, fighter tactics and early warning merely laid a foundation for the aerial phase of training. All of Chennault's pilots needed some familiarization with the P-40, since none of them had flown it before. Even Boyington had difficulty learning the heavy and powerful Tomahawk. On his first attempt he tried to land the plane Navy style, tail low, as though groping for an arrester cable stretched across the deck of an aircraft carrier, and the stiff main landing gear sent him leaping back into the air. After bounding along the asphalt for a few hundred feet, he realized he was headed onto the rain-drenched turf where he was certain to flip over. He opened the throttle wide, but manifold pressure increased so rapidly that the Allison engine almost exploded. He did manage to avoid cracking up, however, and from then on he always landed tail high, touching down with the main gear and then losing momentum.

Boyington was not the only one to have problems. One afternoon Chennault saw six of his pilots misjudge the 100-miles-per-hour landing speed of the P-40, float half the length of the runway, then slam down onto the asphalt when they realized they were running out of room, causing serious damage to their aircraft. A seventh plane was disabled when a mechanic, bicycling along the flight line, became distracted by one of the more spectacularly bad landings and plowed into the fabric covered aileron of a parked plane. The afternoon's performance earned the aviators a lecture on landing the Tomahawk. To reinforce his words, Chennault had a white line painted a third of the way up the runway and imposed a $50 fine on anyone who touched down beyond this point.

During training, Chennault limited the number of planes in the air at any one time, thus reducing the likelihood of collision and enabling him to observe every pilot from his perch atop Kyedaw's bamboo control tower. As he watched, he commented on each man's flying, and his secretary, Tom Trumble, made notes on these remarks. Afterward Chennault used this scribbled commentary to show each individual his strong points and shortcomings.

The volunteers began combat training as soon as they had mastered the basic aerobatic maneuvers. Most of them advanced quickly to this more exacting phase of aerial training and soon became qualified for combat. Some did not, however; after four months, Chennault still had 18 aviators that he did not consider ready to fight the Japanese Zero.

While at Toungoo, the group suffered three fatalities. On 8 September, John Armstrong was practicing team tactics with John ("Gil") Bright, another former naval aviator, when their planes collided. Bright parachuted safely, but Armstrong could not escape from the falling wreckage. Two weeks later, Maax Hammer crashed to his death while trying to find the Kyedaw runway in a blinding monsoon downpour. Peter Atkinson was killed when the P-40 he was testing broke up during a power dive, possibly because of a runaway propeller.

In spite of these deaths, the group's spirits rose during the training period, as the men became surer of each other and more confident of the plane they were flying. Responsible in part for this changing attitude was Erikson Shilling, formerly of the Army Air Corps. While passing through the Netherlands East Indies en route to Rangoon, some of the volunteers had examined the Brewster Buffalo, supplied by the United States to the Dutch armed forces. Possibly because they were naval aviators easily impressed by a U.S. Navy design, the Americans liked the stubby little fighter, and upon reaching Toungoo they complained about having to fly the Army P-40 instead of the Buffalo. This talk ended after Chennault arranged a mock dogfight between Shilling and a pilot from a Rangoon-based Royal Air Force squadron that flew the Brewster. The American overwhelmed his opponent, demonstrating that the Tomahawk, though not the best fighter in the world, was infinitely superior to the Buffalo.

The volunteers also found an identity while they were in training at Toungoo. Some of the men, leafing through an old magazine, came across pictures of British Tomahawks, fighting in the Libyan desert, that had sharks' teeth painted on the radiator cowling. They liked the design and decided to adopt it after Shilling, the man who had defeated the Brewster Buffalo, assured them that superstitious Japanese fishermen considered the tiger shark a symbol of bad luck, and with good reason. Overnight the American Volunteer Group became the Flying Tigers, the members con-

Japanese Zero crippled in action at sea

fident they would prove as deadly in the sky as the tiger shark in the sea.

Back in the United States, two officials of the Central Aircraft Manufacturing Company took the Flying Tiger nickname to the Walt Disney studio in Hollywood. During the national emergency, Disney's illustrators frequently created insignia for military units, and they agreed to apply their talents to devising a symbol for Chennault's group. Their creation was a winged tiger leaping upward from the base of the letter V, a representation of the role of the Flying Tigers in China's ultimate victory over Japan. Later, when Chennault began receiving newspaper clippings about the group from his family in Louisiana, he was amazed not only at how the term "Flying Tigers" had caught on but also at how Shilling's tiger shark had become a jungle animal.

The training flights around Toungoo, vital for sharpening skills and building confidence, caused the first of many supply problems that Chennault would face. Hundreds of practice landings consumed the stock of airplane tires at Toungoo, and there was no time to ship replacements from the United States. Help came from an unexpected quarter, the Philippines, where General Douglas MacArthur agreed to release Army tires to Chennault. Joseph Alsop flew to Manila and arranged the details. Admiral Thomas C. Hart, senior U.S. Navy officer in Asian waters, had the tires flown to Singapore in his patrol bombers, and British authorities rushed the cargo to Toungoo.

Scarcely had this problem been resolved than a greater emergency

Sometimes (as here, later in the war) the
tiger was not a shark at all

Japanese tiger: U.S. crewmen examine the tail of a downed Ki 46 reconnaissance plane

arose. One morning before dawn, flashlights pierced the darkness as headquarters clerks went from bunk to bunk shouting and, if necessary, pulling aside the mosquito netting to shake the pilots awake. The day was 8 December 1941, west of the international date line. Japanese airmen had attacked Pearl Harbor.

If he were a Japanese commander, Chennault reasoned, he would follow up the Hawaii strike by hitting Kyedaw at first light and wiping out Chiang Kai-shek's air arm before it could deploy to defend China. Because he had no warning system in the Toungoo region, the commander decided to get his fighters aloft before the enemy arrived. Taking off in the predawn gloom tested the nerve and ability of the Flying Tigers. Some of the first pilots to reach their planes started down the unlighted runway before their Allison engines had warmed up, rose briefly into the air, then settled back to earth just beyond the asphalt, nosing over and damaging propeller blades. Luckily no one was injured, and the Japanese bombers failed to materialize. The enemy had missed a unique opportunity to deliver a crippling blow. In the weeks that followed he would pay in blood for his error.

# 7. Defending the Gateway to China

Although Japanese bombers failed to deliver the anticipated dawn attack, Chennault knew that the Flying Tigers could not remain at Toungoo without risking disaster. Accordingly, he planned to transfer all three squadrons to Kunming, where Chinese coolies were tamping down crushed rock to form a 7,000-foot runway. From this expanded air base and an increasing number of satellite fields, his men could protect the China end of the Burma Road. But the British wanted the group to operate out of Mingaladon, where it could benefit from Manning's radar in defending the Burma end of China's lifeline. Chennault objected to concentrating his force at Rangoon, arguing that radar coverage in Burma was inferior to the kind of observation net that he had set up around Kunming. Manning, he pointed out, depended upon the notoriously unreliable local telephone company for contact between the radar sites and the Mingaladon control center. Yet Chiang Kai-shek realized that Rangoon was essential to the defense of both China and Burma. The Generalissimo therefore directed Chennault to divide his organization, and so the group commander sent one squadron to reinforce the British at Rangoon and the other two to Kunming.

While he was arriving at this decision, Chennault dispatched a reconnaissance mission over Bangkok, Thailand, where the Japanese were es-

Labor-intensive airfield construction: 500 coolies pull a 10-ton roller

tablishing their main base for an advance into Burma. Erik Shilling, the group photo officer, climbed into a P-40 stripped of its guns to save weight for a camera and took pictures from an altitude of 26,000 feet. Escorting him were Ed Rector and Bert Christman in fully armed Tomahawks, but their weapons proved unnecessary, since no Japanese tried to intercept. Enemy aircraft jammed Don Muang airfield, the photos revealed, and mountains of cargo rose from the waterfront docks. A handful of bombers could almost certainly have upset the enemy timetable for conquering Burma, but Chennault had only fighters. All he could do was abandon Toungoo, preserving his squadrons for the defense of Rangoon and Kunming.

Selected for the long, dangerous flight to Kunming were Robert Sandell's First Pursuit Squadron, nicknamed Adam and Eve, and Jack Newkirk's Second Pursuit Squadron, the Panda Bears. Boyington, a member of Adam and Eve, was amazed at the precision with which Sandell navigated, leading both units some 600 miles, threading his way through cloud-covered mountain ranges and finally locating the narrow valley that led the men over three lakes to the Kunming airfield. Sandell accomplished this with only a topographic map. He had no radio beacon, not even an up-to-date weather forecast.

Sandell, Newkirk and other members of these two squadrons took part in the first air battle fought by the Flying Tigers, the confused melee of 20 December that resulted in the destruction of six or more Japanese bombers at the cost of one P-40, Ed Rector's Tomahawk, which ran out of gas and crash-landed.

The defense of Rangoon initially fell to 25 pilots of Hell's Angels—Arvid Olson's Third Pursuit Squadron—and a Royal Air Force contingent flying three dozen Brewster Buffalos. As had been the case at Toungoo, the Japanese proved slow in moving against a vulnerable target. Rangoon remained quiet until 23 December, when air raid sirens began wailing in the early morning darkness. Nothing happened, however, and a second alarm also proved false. Then, about 1100, the sirens sounded again, followed almost immediately by the roar of antiaircraft guns.

Chennault's fears had been realized, for communication between radar stations and the control center at Mingaladon airfield had failed at the outset. The first wave of 18 twin-engine Nakajima medium bombers droned unmolested over Rangoon and dropped their explosives on the docks. By the time the defenders—16 P-40s and 20 Buffalos—were in position, a second formation of about 30 bombers escorted by 20 Army fighters, probably Nakajima Ki 27s, bore down upon them. In an almost suicidal division of labor, the vulnerable Buffalos went after the fighters, leaving the deadlier Tomahawks to attack the bombers.

Two two-plane teams of Flying Tigers made the first diving passes. Remembering the colored circles chalked on a blackboard at Toungoo, Ken

Jernstedt fired a short burst, and a bomber caught fire immediately, demonstrating the kind of vulnerability Chennault had described in his lectures. The group leader had also cautioned that the Nakajima, like the Navy's G4M, carried a stinger in its tail, but despite the warning this kind of weapon may have shot down the P-40 flown by Henry Gilbert, the first Flying Tiger to be killed in aerial combat. Meanwhile, Charley Older destroyed two bombers, one of them exploding when his gunfire detonated the bombs stowed within the fuselage. It was an almost perfect example of the way to exploit enemy weaknesses, as preached by Chennault. The concussion from this blast may have caused the second Tiger fatality of the day, for Neil Martin's fighter, diving past when the Nakajima exploded, tumbled out of control and crashed. Helping avenge the loss of Gilbert and Martin, volunteers Ed Overend and Robert Smith also claimed victories.

Paul Greene was shooting up a bomber when two Ki 27s jumped him. His P-40 had begun breaking up under their fire when he slid back the canopy and parachuted. As he swung like a pendulum beneath the canopy, the two Japanese took turns shooting at him. Although he was not wounded, bullets tore so many holes in his chute that he landed hard enough to injure his back. Luckily, he was able to fly within two days. The squadron needed every pilot on its roster.

This first aerial engagement over Rangoon had been costly for both attacker and defender. The Japanese had lost six bombers and 10 fighters, the British five Buffalos and their pilots, and the Flying Tigers three planes and two pilots in aerial combat, with a fourth P-40, flown by George McMillan, demolished in a crash landing. Although enemy losses were more numerous, the Japanese had hundreds of modern aircraft to hurl into the fight, while the British and American allies were desperately stripping wrecks for spare parts and patching any aircraft that seemed flyable.

The original plan for the American Volunteer Group had called for the Central Aircraft Manufacturing Company to repair the P-40s either in its workshops at Loi-Wing, in China, or at Chennault's air bases. The Loi-Wing plant, operated by William Pawley, also had a contract with Curtiss-Wright to assemble CW-21 interceptors sold to the Chinese. When Chennault began calling upon Central Aircraft Manufacturing to repair planes damaged in training at Toungoo or shot up in combat, Pawley had to turn him down because the Loi-Wing facility was operating at capacity and he had neither space nor mechanics to spare. Chennault was furious, arguing that proven combat planes like the Tomahawk should take precedence over second-line aircraft like the CW-21, which had all the failings of the Zero fighter and none of its strong points. Eight years later, when he prepared his autobiography, Chennault had not forgiven Pawley for what the leader of the Flying Tigers considered "a remarkable lack of cooperation."

William Pawley, the object of Chennault's anger, was at Rangoon as the Japanese air offensive gathered momentum. The first day's bombing

Arvid Olson, leader of the Hell's Angels squadron

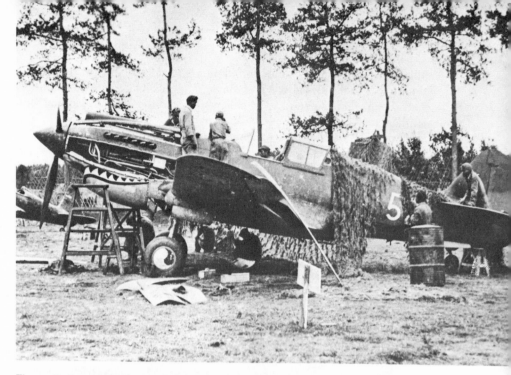

The early days: ground crew works amid primitive facilities

started vast fires on the docks and sent many native stevedores scurrying into the countryside, but the emergency services organized by the British extinguished the flames and restored order among the nervous citizenry. The calm, however, lasted fewer than 48 hours.

The Japanese returned on Christmas Day—though it scarcely seemed like Christmas to Americans used to snow and fir trees instead of 100-degree temperatures and banyans—sending 60 bombers escorted by 30 fighters. Since he had lost confidence in British radar, Olson launched three planes to serve as aerial pickets and sound the alarm if they sighted the enemy. Thanks to their warning, a dozen of Olson's P-40s, joined by 16 Buffalos, intercepted the attackers short of the city. The Flying Tigers broke up this first formation, with Charley Older, Tom Haywood and Duke Hedman shooting down a bomber apiece. In the confused fighting that ensued, five more Japanese bombers crashed in flames, but the Tigers had to break off the action and turn to meet another arriving formation.

The second force, consisting of 20 bombers and eight fighters, melted away before the fire of Hell's Angels, losing three bombers and three fighters. Duke Hedman shot down a Ki 27 and two more bombers. Robert Smith and his partner made a long pass at a Nakajima bomber, diving low behind the victim and zooming upward. Smith's first burst penetrated the bomb-bay doors, and the aircraft exploded with a force that drove fragments from cylinder heads into Smith's engine cowling. Parker Dupouy collided with a Japanese fighter but limped safely home to Mingaladon minus a four-foot piece of wing. Hedman, after his final victim, a second Ki 27, had exploded, nursed his Tomahawk back to the airfield, landing with less than a gallon of fuel in his tanks.

Two P-40s did not return. Some of Olson's Hell's Angels had seen Ed Overend's fighter fall out of the battle, and George McMillan, who had managed to crash-land his battered Tomahawk after the 23 December fight, had disappeared. The British, meanwhile, had lost nine more Buffalos and six pilots, further evidence of the Tomahawk's superiority to the Brewster.

A pair of senior Allied officers, General Sir Archibald Wavell and Major General George H. Brett, U.S. Army Air Forces, almost joined the casualty list. As the Chinese DC-3 bringing them from Chungking on a tour of inspection rolled to a stop at Mingaladon, a Flying Tiger ran onto the apron and shepherded the two officers to a bomb shelter. No raiders appeared, however, and the generals concluded that it was a false alarm. But scarcely had Wavell and his American colleague strolled from the dugout when the bombs began exploding, forcing them to dive for protection into a nearby ditch.

William Pawley had watched the Christmas Day aerial battles as best

Flying Tigers (of the Fourteenth Air Force) answer the air raid signal

he could from a grove of banyan trees near the airfield. Each time a Japanese aircraft crashed to earth, he could see a cloud of greasy smoke billowing upward. The performance of the Flying Tigers so delighted him that he willingly paid inflated prices to send Olson's men a panel truck loaded with ham, chicken, cold beer and Scotch whisky. Their cooks had fled the bombing, two days earlier, and the Tigers had been living mainly on stale bread and warm beer. No matter how Chennault might feel toward him, Pawley was a hero at Rangoon.

Though he missed the Christmas feast that Pawley had provided, Ed Overend came back alive. He had dived away from a Ki 27 that jumped him from behind only to discover that his badly damaged P-40 did not have fuel enough to reach the base. He spotted a swamp, made a smooth wheels-up landing and waded to dry ground. A group of sickle-waving peasants surrounded him, but upon realizing he was not Japanese, they helped him make his way to Mingaladon.

McMillan arrived on the following day, climbing from a bullock cart and limping into squadron headquarters. He had parachuted from his crippled fighter, injured an ankle when he landed and spent the night wandering in the jungle. After daybreak he had come upon the cart that had brought him to the airfield.

The loss of a half-dozen P-40s and mortal damage to several others reduced Olson's force to just 11 combat-ready planes. Chiang raised no objection when Chennault decided to reinforce Hell's Angels with Newkirk's Panda Bears. This deployment was completed during the first week of January 1942, bringing Flying Tiger strength at Rangoon to about 35 airplanes.

While Newkirk's squadron moved southward, E. H. Alexander, an Army Air Forces colonel who would assume responsibility for flying cargo across the Himalayas to China, completed an inspection tour of the theater of operations. Alexander was impressed by the accomplishments of Chennault's fliers and recommended reinforcing the group with Army airmen. "The P-40 flown by American pilots," he told General Arnold, "is superior to the Jap Zero type fighter under combat conditions to date."

Though Alexander did not spell out the reasons for this success, it was obvious that Chennault's training methods and leadership had contributed to the victories being won by his men. Another factor, besides the daring and skill of the individual aviators, had to be the rugged construction of the P-40. Dupouy, for instance, had sideswiped a Ki 27, demolishing it, and yet brought his Tomahawk back safely. Dents in cockpit armor plate proved that this protection, missing from enemy fighters, had already saved the lives of at least three Flying Tigers—McMillan, Overend and Older.

Colonel Alexander's enthusiasm for the Flying Tigers did not carry over to the Chinese air arm. "The current objective of the Chinese Air

Force," he reported to General Arnold, "is to *avoid* combat. They have no will to fight but an almost desperate determination not to fight." This attitude stemmed, he believed, from the "superiority in numbers, armament, and flying equipment of the Jap air force."

His knowledge of Chiang's ground forces was less thorough, but Alexander was equally harsh in judging them. He advised Arnold that China's army "*will not take the offensive.* It will not fight effectively on the defensive, except in guerrilla operations."

As a specialist in delivering cargo by air, Alexander expressed concern about the capacity of the Burma Road. Like other American observers, he summoned up the specter of corruption, warning his commanding general that "60% of the supplies leaving Rangoon for Chungking are reported consumed or lost en route." This massive leakage was easily explained, he believed: "Local politicians, thieves, provincial governors, and the Chinese managerial staff of the Burma Road all take a cut from the traffic." The only solution lay in having the U.S. or British Army operate the road, but even so, he warned, it could "never furnish the tonnage of supplies to China to support any but a token air operation unless the total capacity of the road is devoted to that operation."

Chennault's airmen now defended both ends of China's rail-and-highway lifeline. While Newkirk was going to Olson's aid, the Adam and Eve squadron, commanded by Bob Sandell, was becoming the toast of Kunming. The fighting there remained sporadic compared with the sustained battle over Rangoon, but several of these Tigers received an introduction to aerial combat. Louis Hoffman's first battle after more than 20 years of flying fighters ended in frustration when his guns jammed. He nevertheless made repeated passes at the enemy formation, hoping to create opportunities for his wingman.

Crowds of children tagged along behind Hoffman and the others whenever the Americans visited the city of Kunming. Mme. Chiang made a speech to the squadron, pleading with the Flying Tigers never to lose face against the Japanese. When Arvid Olson, at Rangoon, heard about this admonition, he said that he preferred losing face to losing his ass and intended to act accordingly.

Scarsdale Jack Newkirk's recently arrived Panda Bears scarcely had time to consider Olson's advice before the Japanese resumed their battering of Rangoon. Radio failure plagued the squadron's first attempt to intercept. The communication gear in the Tomahawks, designed originally for light sport planes, could not pick up messages from the Royal Air Force control center, though the controllers could hear what the pilots were saying. Fortunately, the Panda Bears could also talk among themselves once they were airborne. Unable to benefit from radar on the ground, Newkirk stumbled onto the enemy strike force, 40 bombers and 20 Ki 27 fighters boring through a hazy sky. He warned his own squadron and alerted the

Crew readies a P-40 for a mission

Mingaladon controllers, who guided 10 war-weary Buffalos into position to intercept.

The Panda Bears, whose aircraft had this symbol painted near the cockpit, followed Chennault's instructions, fighting in pairs, making a diving pass through the fighter escort and the bombers below, breaking away and climbing to regroup. After the first pass, Newkirk's men could see four of the enemy trailing smoke and plunging toward the ground, but before the Americans could regroup, the Ki 27s pounced upon them. Chennault's lectures again paid off, for the Panda Bears avoided dogfighting the more maneuverable enemy and dived upon him after he had hurtled past. Armor and self-sealing fuel tanks helped make the difference between victory and death, as Newkirk's men escaped injury or serious damage to their aircraft, then followed the Japanese fighters in a gentle 10,000-foot dive, making eight kills in rapid succession. Scarsdale Jack shot down two, Frank Lawlor three, and three others disintegrated before the guns of Tex Hill, Bob Layher and Gil Bright.

While the squadron was polishing off the fighter escort, the bombers made leisurely runs, pounding the docks, the railroad station and Mingaladon airfield. Now, with the Ki 27s either shot down or fleeing, the Tigers hurled themselves at the raiders. The Japanese bomber crews proved as courageous as Chennault had predicted; pilots dived to treetop height, and gunners tried to outshoot the six machine guns in the P-40s with their

Chennault conducts a Chinese commission on a tour at Fourteenth Air Force headquarters

single manually operated weapons. The results were predictable, however. Ed Rector, Tom Cole, Noel Bacon and Fred Hodges scored victories, though hostile fire cut Bert Christman's Tomahawk to pieces, forcing him to bail out.

When the Panda Bears arrived over the airfield, their ammunition gone and the wind whistling through the gun ports where protective tape had been blown away, another group of Japanese bombers was vanishing in the distance. Craters scarred the runways, tool sheds lay in ruins and flames were consuming the base headquarters building. In spite of all this destruction, an enthusiastic Flying Tiger, fresh from his first victory, buzzed the airdrome and executed a triumphant roll. Upon landing, however, he was confronted by a gruesome sight. Displayed on the parking apron was a human head, ripped from the body of a Japanese pilot when he had dived his burning plane onto the pavement in an attempt to ram a parked Bristol Blenheim, one of a handful of bombers the British had recently flown to Mingaladon.

In the space of a few weeks, the Flying Tigers had fired the imagination of the people of Rangoon. Newspapers that had once complained about American ruffians now lavished scarce ink and newsprint on their exploits. Some British residents, however, continued to find the Flying Tigers annoying. These Americans, after all, appeared at exclusive clubs wearing khaki shorts and open-neck shirts, escorting Burmese girls, even though informal attire and the presence of all but the wealthiest natives had always been forbidden.

The Americans cared nothing for dress codes or social custom; their main interest was relaxing after the daily air battle. Once again the Silver Bar became their headquarters, even though liquor was running short and the dinner menu offered nothing but vegetables. As the days passed, finding a few cans of sardines became reason enough for a party.

The care and feeding of Flying Tigers was a minor problem in the overall Allied effort against Japan. After crawling from the ditch at Mingaladon, where he had taken refuge from Japanese bombs during the Christmas Day raid, General Brett toured Rangoon, then headed for Australia, where he wrote a report for General Arnold. His opinions about the China theater, formed during visits to Chungking and Rangoon, reinforced Colonel Alexander's generally pessimistic views.

"My experiences in China," Brett told Arnold, "were anything but pleasant." While at Chungking, Brett and Wavell had conferred with Chiang Kai-shek and Mme. Chiang. This meeting marked Brett's introduction to Chinese politics, and he found it disheartening. Whenever the westerners raised questions of broad policy, the Generalissimo seemed determined to haggle over details, always trying to improve China's bargaining position, and when the discussions concerned minor points, the Chinese leader wanted to talk about major issues. "Madame Chiang sat next to the General," Brett reported, "and her attitude was to become angry whenever the conference did not go in accordance with the General's desire." The American officer complained to Arnold that "the entire conference was purely for the purpose of trying to make a Napoleon out of General Chiang." Absent from Brett's letter was any realization that the Generalissimo hated being dependent upon foreigners and that he might be using his considerable bargaining skill to enhance both his own prestige and the importance of China.

Brett also complained about corruption and mismanagement. He said that most of the Americans he had talked with "felt the Chinese were running a racket and making the most of an opportunity to line their pockets with American gold." In support of this judgment, he passed along reports of cargo lost or misappropriated and testified that he "personally saw large stores of equipment which, I understood, had been in Burma for months."

Like many Americans, he failed to understand that in China graft became a part of every business deal. What Brett considered corruption was normal commercial practice in China. Nor was the backlog of cargo necessarily the result of mismanagement, for no matter how efficient their operators, neither Burma's railways nor the road across the mountains could move cargo as quickly as it could be unloaded at Rangoon. In addition, many of the laborers who moved supplies from ship's hold to warehouse to railroad car had fled the city when Japanese bombs began falling.

Unaware of Chiang's tenuous hold over the army, Brett criticized the Generalissimo for refusing to deploy ground forces to Rangoon. The Nationalist leader, however, dared not dilute his own military strength in the face of possible opposition within China, and he lacked the authority to order some nominal subordinate to run a similar risk.

Brett, in fact, did not believe the Chinese could become combat soldiers. Citing the "filth and dirt in which the Chinese live" and their inability to organize, he concluded that "their main use . . . would be as labor battalions." He advised General Arnold that "if Japan is to be approached from China, it must be done by European and American troops."

While Brett was arriving at these doleful conclusions, the battle for Rangoon continued. A handful of planes and pilots from Sandell's squadron reinforced the Flying Tigers based at Mingaladon. More welcome than the men or aircraft were the turkeys and other food—gifts from a Chinese general—that they brought with them. By way of appreciation, the Tigers collected $1,700 for the care of Chinese war orphans.

The defenders of Burma could not remain exclusively on the defensive while Japanese troops massed along the border with Thailand. As a result, the Flying Tigers threw a counter-punch. On the morning of 3 January 1942, Newkirk, Noel Bacon, and Tex Hill flew the width of the Burma panhandle to attack the enemy airfield at Tak in Thailand.

Parked below them as they approached were row upon row of Japanese planes, precisely aligned, fueled and armed. So tempting was this sight that Newkirk dived to the attack without looking behind him. Luckily, Hill and Bacon did look, and they spotted seven Japanese fighters which they immediately engaged. Newkirk roared low over the field, firing at the parked aircraft, while a Ki 27, guns blazing, pursued him. Bacon dived after this Japanese plane and splattered it all over the runway, while Hill downed a fighter that had started after Bacon. Meanwhile, a squad of enemy soldiers materialized at the end of the runway and opened fire with rifles at the P-40s screaming toward them. A few bursts by Newkirk and Bacon scattered the men. Once again the durable construction of the Tomahawk had saved lives. Hill limped home leaking fuel, but his rubberized tanks had not exploded. Newkirk not only had not seen the enemy fighters but did not realize he had been fired on until he landed at Mingaladon, where Hill pointed out two dozen holes in Scarsdale Jack's aircraft.

This sudden offensive thrust occurred at a time when both the Allies and the Japanese were adjusting their tactics. Because Mingaladon offered an easy target, Rangoon's defenders began dispersing their squadrons among several hurriedly built auxiliary fields. The enemy, in the meantime, paid tribute to the Anglo-American fighter units by abandoning daylight bomber attacks in favor of night raids. Japanese plans now called for daytime fighter sweeps to whittle away Allied defensive strength, followed by area bombing after dark.

Ultimately the Americans carried out raids against targets like this railroad repair shop in Indochina

With neither searchlight batteries nor airborne radar, the Flying Tigers nevertheless tried to intercept the night raiders. Pilots took off either by moonlight or by following a flare path that marked the edge of the runway. Climbing high above the forest, the Americans groped through the blackness in hopes of seeing engine exhaust, cockpit lights or perhaps an indistinct silhouette in the half-light.

One night, three Tigers parked a borrowed car beside the runway to wait for a patrolling fighter to land. While one of them fell asleep in the back seat, the other two sat in front, listening for the approaching P-40 to throttle back, then straining to catch sight of the aircraft. They could see a vague shape against the stars but lost it in a background of trees. When they saw the plane again, it was headed directly toward their automobile. The men on the front seat leaped out, one from each door, and ran for their lives; the Tiger in back may have awakened, but too late, for the propeller killed him.

Although unable to halt the nighttime nuisance raids, the Flying Tigers had helped stop the more destructive daylight bombing. The resulting calm encouraged farmers to bring meat and produce to town, and the Silver Bar once again served steak, though the liquor supply continued to diminish. The improved diet boosted group morale—and so did a series of attacks on enemy airfields, sudden thrusts patterned after the strafing of Tak by Newkirk, Bacon and Hill.

On 9 January, for instance, these three men—plus Pete Wright, Percy Bartlett and six RAF pilots flying recently arrived Hawker Hurricanes—paid a return visit to Tak, shooting up 24 parked planes, three trucks and most of the buildings. On the following morning, Newkirk, Tex Hill and Jim Howard returned to mop up. The mission almost proved fatal to Howard, a veteran of the 20 December air battle at Kunming. While he was firing at a Japanese fighter caught circling to land, his plane's electrical system failed, the engine promptly quit and Howard faced the prospect of a dead-stick landing deep in hostile territory—unless the Ki 27 closing in from behind should shoot him down first. Tex Hill destroyed the enemy plane, Howard's engine came to life and all three of the volunteers got safely away after accounting for a total of five Japanese aircraft.

Chennault took advantage of the comparative lull to send the balance of Sandell's squadron to Rangoon in exchange for the surviving Hell's Angels. If Olson's men expected rest at Kunming, they were disappointed, for within a few days after their arrival the Japanese again attacked. The Tigers intercepted, however, and downed three bombers.

Meanwhile, the two squadrons in Burma were taking part in their most ambitious strike of the war thus far. Newkirk and five other members of his unit escorted six twin-engine RAF Blenheims, which successfully

General Chennault directs operations during a Japanese attack

bombed Meshot, Thailand, even though jumped by seven Ki 27s. Newkirk and Bob Neale scored two kills and two probables between them. Once more, Bert Christman emerged from the battle with his P-40 shot full of holes, but again he survived, this time blowing out a tire when he landed at Mingaladon. Two days later, Christman's luck ran out; he was machine-gunned to death while parachuting from a disabled Tomahawk.

Attacks upon airfields like Tak and Meshot inconvenienced the enemy but could not stop him. He enjoyed the advantage of numbers to begin with, and the daylight fighter sweeps were wearing down the defenders. Gregory Boyington, who arrived with Sandell's second contingent, found that the Japanese would dispatch a blanket of 40 or 50 Ki 27s and dare the Flying Tigers to attack. As the Americans approached, the enemy would open his formation, enabling the stubby fighters to elude the Tigers' pass and outmaneuver any Tomahawk that tried to turn with them. The Japanese hoped to lure the Tigers into a series of individual dogfights in which maneuverability proved decisive.

These tactics sometimes worked. Louis Hoffman, for one, tried to lead an attack on such a formation, approaching it from below. He was almost within firing range, when several of the intended victims flipped onto their backs, executed tight half-loops, and converged on him. As Boyington recalled in his autobiography, Hoffman's plane "resembled a fish writhing in agony out of water" before it spun to earth, killing the veteran pilot.

Boyington himself made a similar mistake but survived. He was diving to the attack, when his quarry slipped out of his sight ring. A touch of aileron corrected the picture, but only for a split second. Boyington persisted and found himself following the enemy through a dizzying series of turns, almost losing consciousness and failing to get the aircraft back in his sights. He was so skilled at aerobatics, however, that his opponent was no more successful in drawing a bead on him. Convinced at last that the odds lay overwhelmingly with the enemy, Boyington nosed over and dived to safety.

By late January the balance had shifted in favor of the Japanese, who now felt they could challenge the Allied fighters by resuming the daylight bombardment of Rangoon. Chennault had planned to fly to Mingaladon for the showdown but fell ill with a return of chronic bronchitis. The critical phase of the air battle for Burma found him confined to a sickbed at Kunming.

The first of a new series of daylight raids came on 23 January. Newkirk and four other Panda Bears intercepted a force of 10 bombers and 12 fighters over the Gulf of Martaban and dropped seven of the bombers into the water. When the enemy returned later in the day, the Flying Tigers shot down 21 out of 50, with John Petach scoring three victories.

Not even a surprise bombing attack could stagger a confident and well-equipped foe. The Chinese Air Force rounded up several Russian-built SB-

2 medium bombers, arranged for an escort from Hell's Angels and bombed the airfield at Hanoi. The daring raid scarcely bothered the Japanese.

Savage fighting continued over Rangoon, where Zero fighters had entered the fray. Raymond Hastey tangled with seven and managed to damage one before enemy fire disabled his plane. As smoke filled the cockpit, he flipped the Tomahawk on its back, opened the canopy, released his seat harness and let himself fall. Remembering how Bert Christman had died a few days earlier, he delayed opening his chute, risking one kind of death to avoid another. The earth was leaping toward him when from the corner of his eye he saw a P-40 circling nearby. With Gil Bright at hand to protect him, he could open his parachute and descend safely.

January gave way to February, and the Flying Tigers strafed Japanese columns advancing from Thailand, escorted British Blenheims and battled enemy formations attacking Rangoon. From London, Prime Minister Winston Churchill lauded the accomplishments of Chennault's group. "The magnificent victories they have won over the paddy fields of Burma," he declared, "may well prove comparable in character, if not in scale, with those won over the orchards and hop fields of Kent in the Battle of Britain."

Air Vice Marshal D. F. Stevenson, the RAF commander in Burma, had already credited the Flying Tigers with 100 confirmed victories, each one attested to either by an eyewitness or by the discovery of wreckage. Many other victims had crashed at sea, buried themselves in rice paddies or plunged into impenetrable jungle. The number of Flying Tigers killed in action had risen to five—Henry Gilbert, Neil Martin, Bert Christman, Louis Hoffman and Thomas Cole—and seven others had died in accidents, including Bob Sandell, killed while testing a P-40 that had undergone repair at Mingaladon.

The skill and courage of the Flying Tigers and their Royal Air Force comrades exacted a heavy toll from the enemy but could not prevent his advance toward Rangoon. In anticipation of the city's fall, ground crewmen loaded damaged aircraft and salvageable equipment on flatcars for shipment northward, and the pilots carried on as best they could. Aircraft tires had worn paper thin, batteries could hold a charge no longer than a day, and the supply of coolant for the Allison engines was running out. This powerplant turned out to be more reliable and easier to maintain than Chennault had believed possible, but the dust at Mingaladon was so thick that mechanics had to disassemble and clean all carburetors after each day's flying. The maintenance crew could barely keep a handful of fighters in action.

Within the city itself chaos reigned. The daily bombing set massive fires that burned out of control. Law enforcement collapsed, jailers emptied the prisons so that the convicts would not be killed by errant Japanese bombs, and looters roamed the streets.

As the enemy closed in, Chennault began pulling his men out of Rangoon. On 8 February, two days after escorting a Blenheim strike against Japanese concentrations along the Salween River, Newkirk received orders to divide the remnants of his squadron among Magwe in Burma and Kunming and Loi-Wing in China. Bob Neale, who had taken over the First Pursuit Squadron after Sandell's death, assumed responsibility for protecting Rangoon with a dwindling number of airplanes. He had only seven battered P-40s when, on 25 February, a message arrived from Kunming. "Conserve materiel and personnel," Chennault instructed him. "Retire from Rangoon on last bottle of oxygen."

Twice that day Neale's men took off to intercept Japanese raiders. Since the British had begun shipping the valuable Rangoon radar set to a safer place, the city's defenders seldom received more than a few minutes' warning. The volunteers nevertheless downed four Zeros in the morning and another 19 aircraft later in the day. Bob Neale scored three of the afternoon's victories and claimed another plane probably destroyed. Two of the seven Flying Tigers failed to return from this second mission of the day, but one of them appeared that evening.

Jim Cross, wounded in the head and shoulders, managed to land safely at an auxiliary field and make his way back to Mingaladon. Ed Liebolt was

Tiger aces include Johnny Alison (inboard on wing) and John Hampshire (second from r. on ground), top China ace at the time of his death

not so lucky. Although his wingman reported seeing him make a successful crash landing, Liebolt did not return, and Neale decided to postpone his own departure as long as possible, in the hope that the missing airman would appear.

Since some oxygen remained, these Flying Tigers took to the air once more, shooting up enemy planes at the Moulmein airfield. During the strafing attack, Japanese Zeros suddenly materialized, and the Americans had to fight their way back to Rangoon. Although Neale scored no victories on this mission—Zeros had chased him into a friendly cloud bank near Moulmein—the total bag claimed for the day was 20 enemy planes shot down or destroyed on the ground.

With no oxygen, very little fuel and no assistance from radar, Neale at last gave up. While the other survivors headed north, he removed the radio from behind his seat, increasing baggage capacity to make room for Liebolt, if the downed flier should return. The squadron leader and R. T. ("Snuffy") Smith, his wingman, spent almost two days waiting in vain. With Japanese forces on all sides of the city, Neale loaded two cases of whisky into the space he had saved for Liebolt and took off with Smith for the RAF base at Magwe.

# 8. Time Runs Out

Ironically, on the very day that Neale and Snuffy Smith pulled out of Mingaladon airfield the Flying Tigers at Kunming were having a celebration. The Generalissimo and Mme. Chiang Kai-shek attended a banquet in the group's dining hall, where they paid tribute to Chennault and his aerial warriors. Chiang, his remarks hurriedly translated from the Chinese, declared that the "splendid victories the Volunteer Group has won in the air are a glory that belongs to China and our ally, America, alike." Men like the absent Bob Neale had "written in the history of this world war a remarkable page, the memory of which will be in our minds forever."

Mme. Chiang addressed the men in her flawless English, lauding Chennault as an "admirable commander" who had "dinned into your ears the necessity for discipline in the field." This external discipline was not enough, she declared. "We must have inner discipline so that we may have fully developed characters." She paused for a moment to study the faces turned toward her. "However," she added, "I am not trying to make you into little saints."

On this evening, the Flying Tigers did show a kind of self-discipline, remaining courteous, attentive and sober, even though Chinese wines and Scotch whisky graced the table. Their restraint may have resulted from the

Bob Prescott, ace who went on to found the civilian Flying Tiger Line

ceremony that preceded the speeches. Chiang had presented posthumous decorations to two of the most popular members of the group, Louis Hoffman and Bob Sandell, both of whom had died at Rangoon.

The respectful attitude did not last, as the Generalissimo's party discovered while preparing to board a DC-2 transport for the flight back to Chungking. Chennault, naturally enough, wanted to impress his distinguished visitors and chose Harvey Greenlaw, his executive officer, to arrange a fly-over. Greenlaw selected a seven-man escort and simply told the pilots to take off, form up at 3,000 feet, and put on a good show. As a result, the fly-over almost became a fly-through, as the men executed the mission with reckless enthusiasm. They did a half-roll while skimming across the airfield, thundering upside down toward the parked transport. Looking back on the incident, Boyington conceded that he and his fellow Tigers "overdid it," for they were so low that the urge for self-preservation sent the official party—including Chiang, his wife and Chennault—sprawling on the ground.

At last the door in the side of the DC-2 slammed shut, the engines bellowed and the plane taxied to the end of the runway. At this point, having noticed that a door on his fighter had come loose, the leader of Chiang's Tiger escorts signaled Boyington to take over. Fresh from Rangoon, where he had claimed four kills during the final weeks of the fighting, Boyington led his patrol toward Chunking, watching for Japanese fighters so that he could protect the transport and, if possible, also increase his total of aircraft destroyed.

As the DC-2 and its escort crossed the mountains separating Kunming from Chungking, clouds gathered and a stiff headwind began blowing. Boyington realized that his fighters did not have fuel enough to butt their way through to Chiang's capital, but he also knew that Japanese fighters could never find the transport amid the thickening clouds, so he ordered the escort to follow him either to Kunming or to one of its satellite airfields. The wind now pushed the Tomahawks southward but could not compensate for the excessive amount of gasoline burned earlier. The P-40s broke out of the clouds well short of the nearest airfield with their tanks almost dry.

Below them lay a burial ground, the only flat space in sight, and one at a time the six planes landed wheels up on the grass surface. After the last Tomahawk had skidded to a stop, Boyington radioed Kunming to report what had happened and ask that someone come for them. Harvey Greenlaw answered and thought for a moment. In the space of a few hours, Boyington's flight had buzzed China's first family, embarrassing the group commander, and crash-landed a half-dozen valuable airplanes. His reply was succinct: Don't come back.

But return they did, hitching a ride with a Chinese truck driver who cheerfully careened along the twisting roads, making two-wheel turns at the edge of 1,000-foot precipices. The Americans tried everything short of assault and battery to get hold of the wheel, but the driver would not surrender his vehicle. He even found room for a couple of Chinese soldiers, one of whom became violently carsick and vomited over an already angry Flying Tiger. Had his fellow airmen not intervened, the Tiger would certainly have strangled the unfortunate trooper.

For Boyington, getting back to Kunming was just a beginning. Since he was responsible for losing the airplanes, he felt obliged to retrieve them. A few mechanics accompanied him back to the cemetery, examined the planes and decided that four of them could be flown out. The mechanics extended landing gears, straightened propellers and hammered out dents in wings and fuselages. They removed guns and radios, then poured 30 gallons of gasoline into each craft. Boyington opened the engine of the first plane as wide as he dared, roared across the flat space, and staggered into the air. Within sight of the nearest airstrip, an auxiliary field at Mengtzu, he ran out of fuel but managed to glide to a safe landing. He climbed into a light plane, was flown back to the graveyard and brought back a second P-40. At this point Greenlaw called off the recovery effort, possibly because he felt Boyington's luck was about to run out.

While the former marine was retrieving the two P-40s, the war shifted from the Rangoon area to the wilds of northern Burma, and it underwent a

Chinese-Americans work on a P-40 at Kunming

basic change. "The battles over Rangoon were deliberate clashes between the two air groups at altitude, both seeking a decision in the air," Chennault explained in his autobiography. "Over northern Burma the character of the battle shifted to continual attempts to catch the opposition on the ground and shooting sitting ducks."

During the fight for northern Burma, the main Allied base was Magwe, its southwestern approaches covered by the radar set brought north from Rangoon. No ground observers complemented the radar, but a Blenheim picket plane usually kept watch for bombers approaching from Thailand. Besides Magwe, the Flying Tigers and the British remnants also operated from Loi-Wing and the old training base at Toungoo.

Vulnerable though it was, Toungoo served as refueling points for a mission that delivered a damaging blow to the Japanese squadrons based around Moulmein. On 19 March, Bill Reed and Ken Jernstedt took off from Magwe, refilled their tanks at Toungoo and headed toward Moulmein airfield on an armed reconnaissance flight. About 10 miles from their goal they saw a new airstrip with 20 fighters parked wingtip to wingtip. The two men executed six strafing runs without drawing antiaircraft fire and set fire to 15 A6M Zeros. Hugging the treetops, they flew to the main airdrome, making one quick pass that resulted in the destruction of a transport and three bombers. Since enemy gunners now were manning their weapons and trying to track the P-40s, a second pass would have been suicidal. In roughly five minutes, Reed and Jernstedt had shared in the destruction of 19 enemy planes.

On the following day the British tried their hand at shooting sitting ducks. Blenheims escorted by Hurricanes flew from Magwe to Mingaladon, where they bombed and strafed 50 Japanese aircraft. Surprise was not complete, however; several Zeros got into the air and inflicted at least minor damage on most of the Blenheims. The Japanese lost a dozen Zero fighters and 16 bombers, all of them destroyed on the ground.

These two successful raids accounted for 47 enemy planes, but this represented only eight percent of his total aerial strength. The Japanese still outnumbered the combined Flying Tiger–Royal Air Force contingent by 10 to 1. This overwhelming superiority in numbers soon made itself felt.

On 21 March, 20 Zero fighters escorted 10 bombers against Magwe, eluding both the Blenheim picket plane and the ground-based radar. With scarcely a minute's warning, two RAF pilots got into the air, as did three Tigers—Parker Dupouy, Bill Reed and Ken Jernstedt. Dupouy, who had barely escaped death over Rangoon when he had collided with an enemy fighter, joined Reed in attacking the escorting Zeros. Closing from behind, Dupouy opened fire on a straggler, which exploded in his face. Reed, meanwhile, suffered wounds to his face and neck that forced him to land. With Reed out of the fight, a half-dozen Zeros went after Dupouy, firing into the cockpit. Armor plate behind the seat saved his life, but he was hit

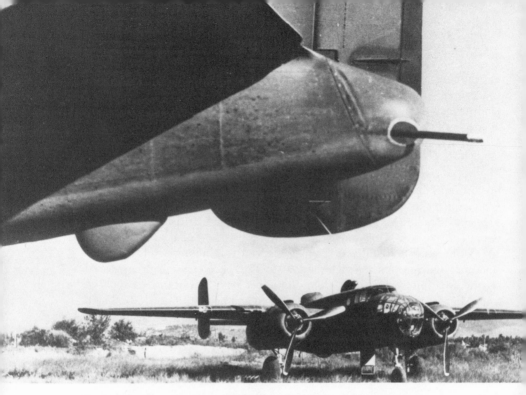

Rear "wobble" gun added to B-25s after combat revealed weakness

in the arms and legs. Even though Japanese bombs had already begun exploding on the airfield, he made a successful landing. Jernstedt plunged into the battle just seconds later, but he, too, was wounded and had to land.

An RAF pilot, trying to land as the raid ended, was less fortunate than the three Flying Tigers. His Hurricane flipped over when it struck a bomb crater and caught fire. Frank Swartz, a pilot in the Hell's Angels squadron, crew chief John Fauth and Bill Seiple, a mechanic, were wounded by bomb fragments while trying unsuccessfully to rescue the trapped aviator. Dr. Lewis Richards, one of the group surgeons, helped drag the wounded Americans to cover and get them to the base hospital where Fauth died the following morning. An ambulance plane evacuated the other two casualties, but only Seiple lived. Swartz died in a Calcutta hospital a month after he had been wounded.

Throughout the afternoon of 21 March, Japanese planes, including G4Ms and escorting Zeros, battered the airfield. When the bombing ended, Magwe lay in ruins, with buildings on fire and the wreckage-strewn runway pockmarked by craters. Eight Tomahawks sustained damage, but only two were beyond repair. The Blenheim force was all but wiped out. Three of them had been loading bombs when the enemy appeared. He scored a direct hit on each of them, and only smoking craters and unidentifiable wreckage remained. Another eight Blenheims sustained mortal damage. The Royal Air Force also lost eight Hurricanes, including the one that had crashed and burned.

Chennault ordered four of the eight flyable Tomahawks to Loi-Wing, leaving Dick Rossi and two wounded pilots, Jernstedt and Dupouy, to help the few surviving Hurricanes defend Magwe. When the Japanese returned without warning on the following day, not a single Flying Tiger managed to get to his plane, let alone take off. A couple of Hurricanes staggered into the air, but a swarm of Zeros shot them down almost immediately. A leisurely bombardment then knocked Magwe out of the war for good. Flying Tiger ground crews loaded the repairable P-40s onto trucks and headed for Loi-Wing.

The retreat first from Mingaladon and then from Magwe had sapped the morale as well as the physical strength of the surviving Flying Tigers. According to Boyington, when Chennault called upon the men at Loi-Wing to attack the Japanese base at Chiengmai, Thailand, he found they were in no condition to carry out his orders. He flew down from Kunming, but after trying a combination of threats and flattery, decided not to force the issue.

Instead, the group commander returned to Kunming, called together his pilots and made a speech that Boyington remembered as "the world's best." He quickly had 10 volunteers for the mission, among them Newkirk, Neale and Boyington. The men flew to Loi-Wing, stayed at quarters maintained for executives and engineers at Pawley's aircraft assembly plant, and went over the attack plan. Neale was to take five men—Boyington, Ed Rector, "Black Mac" McGarry, William Bartling and Charley Bond—stage through the Royal Air Force auxiliary field at Nam Sang, Burma, and strafe Chiengmai. Newkirk, with three Panda Bears, would refuel at Heho, another British airstrip, rendezvous with Neale's flight, and make a nearly simultaneous strike against Lampang airdrome, Thailand.

The two groups took off as planned and landed late in the afternoon at the two forward airfields. Ground crews topped off the gas tanks, and the pilots stretched out beneath the wings of their fighters, resting for a few hours before an 0400 departure. Kerosene flares and truck headlights provided the illumination as the Tomahawks rose from the dirt runways and climbed into the early morning darkness.

The plan began falling apart when the two flights failed to make contact. Neale pushed on to Chiengmai, but when he arrived antiaircraft gunners were already manning their weapons, and the 40 aircraft based there were warming up. Boyington thought the Zeros among them were preparing to intercept the six-man strike group, but the Japanese may have been preparing to launch a raid of their own and simply wanted some fighters aloft at a time when the bombers were especially vulnerable. Whatever their mission, the Zeros did not take off in time; the first pass by Neale's flight set fire to several taxiing aircraft and blocked the runway. Although the antiaircraft fire was the heaviest the Americans had ever experienced, they made three successive passes, destroying an estimated 20 enemy planes.

As Neale shaped a course for Nam Sang, the six pilots closed their formation to check each other for damage. All of them had the usual holes in wings and tail surfaces, and Black Mac's P-40 was trailing smoke. About 55 miles east of the Burma border, he reported that he had no oil pressure and bailed out. The others saw him land safely, but nothing more was heard about him for years—until early in 1945, when agents of the Office of Strategic Services, a precursor of the Central Intelligence Agency, reported he was alive in the Bangkok jail. McGarry had spent almost a month in the jungle before being arrested by Thai security police. Instead of handing him over to the Japanese, who might have executed him, his captors treated him as a civilian, jailing him at Bangkok, where he remained until the local underground rescued him and turned him over to American intelligence.

While Neale's men were shooting up Chiengmai, Scarsdale Jack Newkirk and his formation found Lampang airfield vacated by the Japanese. Deciding to join in the attack on Chiengmai, Newkirk followed the road that linked the two bases, strafing vehicles and buildings en route. He attacked an armored car, which returned the fire. While Newkirk's .303-caliber slugs were rattling off the hardened steel, the enemy gunner scored a direct hit with his light cannon. Scarsdale Jack's P-40 crashed on the roadway, exploded and burned.

Newkirk's death deprived the Flying Tigers of one of their best and most dependable pilots. He had led the Panda Bears in aerial combat and on strafing missions. The record credited him with shooting down 10 Japanese planes and sharing with his wingman in the destruction of an 11th. When he left for the Orient, he had written his wife that the American Volunteer Group was "going to challenge the whole aggressive movement in the Far East." Participating in this challenge had cost him his life.

Although unable to undertake the Chiengmai mission, Olson's squadron was doing an exceptional job defending Loi-Wing. Alerted by a warning network modeled after the one around Kunming, Hell's Angels and the British Hurricanes serving with them usually knew when the enemy was approaching, except on those days when atmospheric conditions interfered with radio communication. On 8 April, for example, 11 P-40s and four Hurricanes were aloft and waiting when 20 Zeros appeared on a fighter sweep; the Allies shot down 10 of the enemy at the cost of two British aircraft. Two days later, however, radio contact failed between observation posts and airfield, allowing 10 Zeros to strafe Loi-Wing unopposed.

The month of April saw the arrival of a handful of new fighters, P-40Es, that were faster and better armed than the Tomahawks. The E models mounted three .50-caliber guns in each wing, had optical gunsights, and boasted fittings for bomb racks and auxiliary fuel tanks. In mak-

General Stilwell commanded ground troops in Burma

ing these improvements, Curtiss engineers had not sacrificed the armor and self-sealing internal tanks that had given the P-40B an advantage over the Zero.

Neither the appearance of the first few P-40Es nor victories by Olson's men at Loi-Wing could stop the Japanese advance. Aerial combat was not enough; Chiang Kai-shek had to call upon Chennault to come to the aid of the Chinese forces retreating before the Japanese in northern Burma. The Generalissimo wanted the Flying Tigers to shoot up road traffic and carry out precise strafing missions in support of defensive positions.

Chiang had given Chennault's group an impossible assignment. The combat zone was poorly mapped, and ground units could seldom make radio contact with the supporting aircraft. Sometimes strafing missions arrived at the specified grid coordinates but could not see the front lines because of the jungle canopy. In order to locate landmarks, pilots had to fly below 10,000 feet, which left them easy prey for Zeros. Moreover, antiaircraft defenses were rapidly improving at road junctions, airfields and other likely targets. Dummy trucks and airplanes served as bait in deadly flak traps, where camouflaged guns waited to fire on any Flying Tiger who tried to attack. These missions were as frustrating as they were dangerous. "There is nothing," Chennault later acknowledged, "that takes the joy out of flying faster than hours and hours of strafing just above the jungle treetops in the face of heavy ground fire."

The fatigue and strain of these missions sapped morale even more rapidly than Chennault suspected. A crisis arose on 20 April, when he issued

Women and children help build a runway

orders for another raid against Chiengmai, where Newkirk and McGarry had been lost. Pilots from Newkirk's old squadron, the Panda Bears, and Olson's Hell's Angels were to escort a flight of Blenheims. Being tied to these lumbering bombers made the prospects for survival seem even gloomier, for the leisurely flight to the target would give the Zero fighters and antiaircraft batteries plenty of time to prepare. Also, many of the Flying Tigers believed their role should be more aggressive, attacking Japanese raiders by gaining altitude, making a diving pass, and climbing to regroup—precisely the tactics Chennault had taught. Now, on Chiang's orders, they were expected to give the enemy the advantage of altitude throughout their approach and during the dangerous minutes when at least some of the P-40s would be strafing the airfield.

Chennault's theories of leadership were undergoing their most severe test. Already, America's entry into the war had persuaded him to adjust his method of discipline. Firings had taken on the trappings of courts-martial, with 27 pilots or ground crewmen having been drummed out of the group since Pearl Harbor. But the commander tried to consult with members of his organization before meting out punishment of any sort, and the fines normally levied for misconduct continued to be decided by panels selected from among the volunteers. In this instance, the threat of fines or even firing was meaningless, for most of the pilots in two veteran squadrons hung poised on the brink of mutiny.

Chennault sympathized with his fliers, but he could not let them defy orders. He, too, felt that the United States had abandoned the Flying Tigers. He was disgusted by the sight of "numerous American Army staff officers scuttling pompously about India and China with briefcases, taking up valuable cargo space . . ." The American Volunteer Group had provided the only aerial victories won thus far in the war against Japan. As a result, everyone seemed eager to visit Kunming, but no one brought help.

One of the pilots based at Loi-Wing drew up a petition declaring that the signers would resign unless the Chiengmai mission was canceled. Twenty-eight Flying Tigers had endorsed the declaration by the time it reached Tex Hill. He got to his feet and pointed out that the rules had changed since Pearl Harbor. No member of the group, even though technically a mercenary in the employ of the Chinese government, could simply walk out on a war in which his own nation, the United States, was involved. He offered to lead the mission, and four other pilots—Ed Rector, Duke Hedman, Frank Schiel and R. J. ("Catfish") Raines—said they would go along. The five pilots took off from Loi-Wing but had to turn back short of Chiengmai when the Blenheims failed to meet them because of bad weather.

Chennault continued his struggle to restore morale, meeting with his dissident pilots, expressing understanding of their views and refusing to interpret the conflict as a personal insult. He reluctantly accepted resignations from the bitterest of the protesters, in all no more than a handful of men. To encourage those who remained, he arranged for President Roosevelt to send a personal letter commending the group for "outstanding gallantry and conspicuous daring" and promising both new equipment and leave, the latter to be granted "just as soon as replacements have absorbed your experience, training, and tradition." In addition, Chennault complained to Mme. Chiang about the misuse of his airmen, and on 23 April the Generalissimo himself replied, agreeing that the Flying Tigers should fight enemy aircraft and not engage in close support of ground troops. In fairness to the men, the group commander felt obliged to warn them that if circumstances forced Chiang or Lieutenant General Joseph W. Stilwell, the senior American commander, to order strafing missions, the Tigers would have to obey.

The best way to restore morale was through aerial victories, such as Olson's men had been winning in defense of Loi-Wing. This town was especially important because Pawley's assembly plant now worked full time repairing the group's P-40s. If Japanese bombers could be kept away from this target, the Central Aircraft Manufacturing Company would be able to repair the wrecks that had been trucked in from Toungoo, Mingaladon or Magwe. The enemy, of course, realized the value of Loi-Wing, and during

U.S. sergeant repairs P-40 instruments

the latter part of April his reconnaissance craft made frequent flights over the city. Obviously, the Japanese were planning something big.

This activity reminded Chennault of events at Hankow in 1938, when enemy airmen had planned a massive offensive to celebrate the Emperor's birthday and flown into a trap sprung by the Russians. He was certain the Japanese had a similar raid in mind for 29 April, the Emperor's birthday, and that the target would be Loi-Wing or the Burmese town of Lashio. On the appointed day he ordered two flights of Tomahawks under Arvid Olson and Tex Hill to patrol near Loi-Wing, while remaining ready to cover Lashio, should it be the enemy objective.

The P-40s had just taken off when Colonel Caleb Haynes of the Air Transport Command touched down at Loi-Wing, leading three C-47s loaded with badly needed munitions. Chennault tried to shoo the Haynes flight back into the air, for if even one Japanese bomber got through and scored a hit on these explosives-laden transports, the resulting blast would put the airfield out of action for good. The colonel, who was understandably reluctant to risk taking off with his trio of winged bombs, sought permission to unload, arguing that the warning net could not have seen an approaching enemy formation because the flagpole for the air raid signal was bare. At that precise moment, according to Chennault, the warning symbol rose slowly up the staff, and Haynes jogged to his C-47, muttering how Chennault must be able to smell enemy bombers.

The Japanese divided their strike force between Loi-Wing and Lashio. Olson sent half his fighters to the defense of the Burmese town and led the others to join Hill's five P-40s. The Zeros escorting the Loi-Wing raiders tangled with the interceptors, which numbered about 10 planes, and the bombers managed to slip through and blast craters that required the rest of the day to fill. This temporary success cost the enemy 22 Zero fighters, 16 shot down near Loi-Wing and the rest over Lashio—hardly the kind of result to delight an Emperor.

Within two days, however, Emperor Hirohito could celebrate the occupation of Loi-Wing, abandoned to the advancing Japanese divisions. The Flying Tigers fell back to Paoshan and Yunnanyi, which Chennault intended to use as outposts while he reorganized the group at Kunming. Unfortunately, the two satellite bases were becoming more vulnerable by the day, for enemy patrols were overrunning the ground observation stations deployed to give warning to aircraft based there.

Proof of this vulnerability came on 4 May, when 50 bombers struck without warning, devastating Paoshan. Ben Foshee was killed by bomb fragments as he sprinted to his plane, and only Charley Bond managed to take off. He caught up with the departing formation and claimed two victims. Zero fighters, however, doubled back, set his P-40 on fire, and forced him to bail out. He landed safely.

Chennault expected the Japanese to return on the following day and

C-47 circles over a remarkably smooth landing field

dispatched nine Tomahawks to Yunnanyi, where they refueled and stood by for further orders. At midmorning, radio operators at Kunming intercepted a message indicating that enemy bombers were taking off from Mingaladon and Chiengmai, bound for Paoshan. The group commander ordered the Yunnanyi contingent to head them off, but the Tigers failed to make contact with the first group of raiders until the attack on the airfield had begun. The P-40s dived on the Japanese, shot down eight Zeros that were strafing Paoshan, then climbed to meet a second hostile formation which immediately fled.

Meanwhile, the Allied ground forces in Burma were taking what General Stilwell described as "a hell of a beating." Unless the retreating Chinese divisions could rally, the Japanese could conceivably advance all the way to Kunming. The dynamiting of a bridge by the Chinese temporarily halted the enemy at the Salween River, but on 7 May Japanese engineers arrived to begin building a pontoon bridge that would enable the attack to continue.

The situation was so desperate that Chennault asked Chiang's permission "to attack targets between Salween and Lungling city." The Generalissimo promptly agreed, and the group commander began planning a strike on the bridge construction site beside the Salween. Although the new P-40Es could carry fragmentation bombs on wing racks, heavier ordnance seemed essential. Luckily, the Chinese Air Force had some 570-pound high-explosive bombs, provided by the Russians for use with the SB-2s. Two Flying Tiger armorers, Charley Baisden and Ray Hoffman, jury-rigged a rack that enabled the E model to carry one of these bombs instead of an auxiliary fuel tank.

Tex Hill, Tom Jones, Ed Rector and Frank Lawlor took off in bomb-laden P-40Es, escorted by Arvid Olson, Snuffy Smith, Erik Shilling and Tom Haywood in B models. En route to the Salween, they sighted a storm looming ahead of them, but the eight men refused to turn back. Hill led the way among the lightning-charged clouds, as rain beat upon the planes and downdrafts sucked them earthward. After a quarter of an hour of battling the weather, they broke out into sunshine and shortly afterward saw the river and the bridge site.

Japanese engineers had begun manhandling the huge pontoons into position at the water's edge when the Flying Tigers appeared overhead. Enemy antiaircraft batteries had been unable to keep pace with the advance, depriving these troops of defense against air attack. As a result, Hill's flight could do its job methodically, first using the Russian bombs to cut the road over which the Japanese had come, so that escape was impossible. Next the Tigers showered fragmentation bombs on the trucks

Tex Hill climbs into his P-40

trapped by the river side. Finally they strafed the pontoons and the men trying to assemble them.

For several days, bombing and strafing continued, with no complaints from the Flying Tigers. Frank Schiel, for example, led a flight of P-40Es toward Lungling, spotted a column of light tanks and dropped more of the Russian-built bombs on them. The savage attack scattered the enemy. The Japanese suffered still another setback when Chennault's men destroyed a truck convoy carrying gasoline to fuel the advance. Until the monsoon rains began falling in mid-May and combat operations bogged down in the mud, the Flying Tigers shot up everything that moved on the roads of enemy-held northern Burma.

Chennault later claimed that his volunteers had "staved off China's collapse." They had certainly helped stop the enemy drive, but time had almost run out on the Flying Tigers. Contracts with the Central Aircraft Manufacturing Company would begin expiring in June, and the total number of combat-ready aircraft seldom reached 50, despite the arrival of a few P-40Es. Chennault himself had been summoned to active duty, promoted to colonel and then to brigadier general. He had already agreed to take orders from Stilwell; all that remained was the formal incorporation of the volunteers and their leader into an American command structure.

General Bissell—Chennault's old antagonist

# 9. Disbanding the Tigers

For the final 90 days of their existence as a unit, the Flying Tigers occupied a unique position. They remained employees of the Chinese government, though earmarked for integration into the U.S. Army Air Forces, and Chennault, now back on active duty, took orders from Chiang Kai-shek, the group's employer, and from Lieutenant General Joseph W. Stilwell, the senior American officer in the area. Early in March 1942—when Stilwell, the recently appointed commander of American forces in China, Burma and India, visited Kunming—Chennault had agreed to take orders from him and to permit his volunteer group to be inducted into the Army Air Forces. This agreement did not specify where Chennault and his organization would fit in the regional command structure or how the Flying Tigers would become Army airmen.

A shadow command structure was already in existence when Stilwell and Chennault conferred. Chosen as senior American air officer was Major General Lewis H. Brereton, with Colonel Clayton Bissell, soon to be promoted to brigadier general, as his principal subordinate. Over the weeks, Bissell had helped organize the "China Aviation Project," which would become the nucleus of the Tenth Air Force. For this program, he and his fellow planners had selected 33 Lockheed A-29s, 37 Consolidated B-24s

Stone-crushing coolies ignore B-24 overhead

commanded by Colonel Harry Halverson, 16 North American B-25s led by Colonel Jimmy Doolittle, and 51 P-40Es. Plans called for the A-29 crews to join the Tenth Air Force after turning their planes, known as Hudsons, over to the Chinese. Halverson's Liberators would bomb Japan from bases in China, the new P-40s were replacements for the Tomahawks flown by Chennault's pilots, and Doolittle's unit was to take off from an aircraft carrier, bomb Japan and then become an element of the Tenth Air Force in China.

As things turned out, the plan collapsed, though through no fault of Bissell's. The P-40Es, delivered by way of Africa, proved slow in reaching their destination. Doolittle's men bombed Japan, but not one of their B-25s landed safely on the mainland. Moreover, the Doolittle raid triggered a Japanese offensive that overran the bases intended for use by Halverson's bombers. As a result, his B-24s—and the A-29s, as well—remained in the Middle East, where Axis forces threatened the Suez Canal. Circumstances had thus deprived the Tenth Air Force of its intended striking power.

Events would prove, however, that the most important aspect of the project was not the unsuccessful effort to create a bomber command but the decision to send 35 C-47 cargo planes. These represented the down payment on the 100 Douglas transports that T. V. Soong had requested of President Roosevelt. He had assured the President that such a fleet could deliver 12,000 tons of cargo a month across the Himalayas into China. The aerial highway foreshadowed by the original 35 transports would have to replace the Burma Road, at least until a new overland route could be built beyond reach of the Japanese.

Although the Japanese conquest of Burma had cut his only reliable rail and highway link with the outside world, Chiang continued to bargain with his usual skill. In return for a promise to cooperate in the transfer of the Flying Tigers to American control, the Generalissimo received an assurance that Chennault, his trusted adviser, would be senior air commander in China. The proposed force structure, however, set up an overall commander for China, Burma and India, placing Chennault in a subordinate role. Although promoted to brigadier general and put in charge of operations within China, he found himself designated as subordinate to Brigadier General Clayton Bissell, who outranked him by one day.

The issue was settled in Washington. Although the command arrangement was not what Chiang had wanted, T. V. Soong endorsed it, apparently without consulting the Generalissimo. Lauchlin Currie, however, visited General Arnold to present Chiang's viewpoint and intercede on Chennault's behalf. The attempt by a presidential aide to influence a military decision infuriated Arnold, who interpreted it as proof that he had decided wisely in nominating Bissell for high command instead of a maverick like Chennault. The successful leader of the American Volunteer Group, an acknowledged master of fighter tactics whose celebrated Flying Tigers had defeated the Japanese Zero, would thus become the subordinate of a man, Bissell, whom he had detested since the two had served at the Air Corps Tactical School in the 1930s.

Tommy Corcoran had been correct when, on the strength of their first meeting, he had concluded that Chennault might prove a difficult subordinate. The commander of the Flying Tigers disliked Bissell and was forming a similar opinion of Stilwell, whom he blamed for refusing to appoint him to a job at least the equal of Bissell's. Currie's attempt to influence Arnold had in fact annoyed Stilwell, and he promptly ratified the decision to place Bissell in charge.

Chennault, who respected Chiang as the living symbol of a free China, also objected to Stilwell's attitude toward the Generalissimo. The Army general insisted that China participate fully in the Allied war effort, with the Generalissimo not only permitting American training cadres to restructure Chinese divisions but also allowing these troops to help recapture Burma. Chiang, however, wanted only arms and training, for he intended to keep his divisions intact for the eventual showdown with the Communists. When the blunt and short-tempered Stilwell tried to exert pressure on the Chinese to fight in Burma, Chennault saw justification for his belief that the Army officer regarded his Oriental allies as "inferiors incapable of managing their own affairs without foreign direction." Stilwell, he declared, had "a complete disregard of the diplomatic facets of a top military post in a coalition war."

Chennault also accused Stilwell of having "a strong prejudice against air power coupled with a faint suspicion of any weapon more complicated than a bayonet." In fact, the senior officer was not so reactionary. True, he emphasized comparatively simple weapons, not excluding artillery, for China's divisions and advocated an overland advance into Burma, but he nevertheless assigned an important supporting role to aviation. Although he did not consider the airplane a decisive weapon, he grasped its importance in carrying troops, protecting and supplying friendly forces and damaging the enemy.

Chennault, in contrast, was coming to the conclusion that air power could defeat the Japanese forces in China. As had been true since his youth in Louisiana, he found it difficult to explain his views and use persuasion on his superiors. Once again, he saw a bigger boy, Stilwell, pushing around the younger ones, the Flying Tigers and the people of China, whom he felt obliged to defend by any means possible. Soon Chennault would begin behaving just the way he had a decade earlier at the Air Corps Tactical School; he would begin overreacting.

Although he unquestionably had the unfortunate habit of seeing a personal attack behind almost every adverse decision, Chennault had good reason to complain about the treatment that his men and the Chinese were receiving. The Flying Tigers seemed to be getting the equipment that was left over after the needs of every other combat theater had been met. Chiang, too, was being asked to survive mainly on promises. In the summer of 1942, for instance, the United States not only diverted the China-bound A-29s and Halverson's B-24s to the Middle East but also summoned Brereton to help meet the crisis that had arisen there.

Nor did Bissell, his fellow airman, seem a likely ally in obtaining reinforcements and equipment. Back in April, while serving as Stilwell's air officer, Bissell had refused to disclose either to Chiang or to Chennault the details of Doolittle's planned attack on Japan. Secrecy had seemed essential to frustrate the network of spies operating in Chungking. Chennault, however, blamed Bissell for keeping him in the dark and preventing him from using his ground observers to communicate with the approaching bombers and guide them to friendly airfields. This conduct, Chennault later declared, "did nothing to alter my opinion of him [formed] when I studied fighter tactics under him at the Air Corps Tactical School in 1931."

As command arrangements clarified and rivalries sharpened, the Flying Tigers kept up the fight even though their contracts were about to expire. The battlefield returned to the skies over Chungking, and Chennault collected the remnants of his group at Peishiyi, about 20 miles from the capital. He dispatched frequent patrols over Chungking, for the benefit of spies in the city. Enemy planes soon reconnoitered Peishiyi and spotted dozens of P-40s, which actually were bamboo-and-cloth dummies built by Chinese laborers. While the Japanese laid plans to attack this airfield, Chennault left four actual P-40s there to maintain the illusion of continued

Colonel Robert L. Scott and Chennault meet at Kunming

activity and transferred the rest to forward bases in east China. From these locations they protected Chungking by attacking ships and airdromes at Canton and Hankow, raids that caused the enemy to call off his air offensive against the capital and concentrate on neutralizing the scattered airstrips. One such strike, against the field at Kweilin, cost the Japanese at least a dozen planes.

Among those who flew these final missions was Colonel Robert L. Scott, USAAF, sent by Bissell to help incorporate the Flying Tigers into the Tenth Air Force. Although Scott had commanded an Army pursuit squadron, when he arrived at Kunming in April he volunteered as a wingman to learn the tactics employed by the Flying Tigers. He ranged over northern Burma, Thailand and eastern China on a series of dangerous missions, shooting up trucks, parked planes and antiaircraft batteries—exploits that earned him the Silver Star.

Scott was flying wingman on a strafing mission in Indochina when antiaircraft fire downed his flight leader, Lew Bishop, a veteran of Tex Hill's attacks on the Salween River pontoon bridge. French authorities in Thailand, who captured Bishop, turned him over to the Japanese. He remained a prisoner of war until 1945, when he jumped from a train carrying him from Shanghai to a prison camp in Manchukuo and eventually made his way to Kunming. While in captivity, he met a Japanese aviator who had fought in the Flying Tigers' first air battle, in December 1941. The Japanese told Bishop that nine of the 10 bombers dispatched against Kunming that day either were shot down or crashed.

The integration of the Flying Tigers into the Tenth Air Force, a process in which Scott was to participate, got off to a poor start. The Navy and Marine Corps pilots knew they would be welcomed back when their China service ended, and some of them began drifting off in anticipation of the group's disbanding. Also departing were the injured and those seeing limited service because of the shortage of planes.

Among those who had decided to return to the services in which they held commissions was Gregory Boyington. After fighting at Rangoon, he had seen action at Loi-Wing and escorted Russian-built Chinese bombers against Hanoi; he received credit for shooting down a total of six planes. He was, however, thoroughly fed up with China, which he considered barbaric and dirty, and he detested Chiang, whom he later described as "nothing but a front for his wife." Mme. Chiang, a fairy-tale princess to Chennault, impressed Boyington as being "a number-one con artist."

Two accidents sidelined the former marine, giving him time to think about his probable fate. The Allison engine of his P-40 quit during a hurried takeoff, and he crash-landed near a tiny village. Bleeding from a gash on the forehead and hobbled by injured knees, he staggered toward some peasants, seeking their help, but they ignored him, further evidence to him of the gulf separating Chinese from American ways. He reinjured his knees when he fell while seeking cover during a night air raid. He eventu-

Scott in his P-40

ally returned to duty, though not to combat, spending his days testing aircraft that had undergone engine overhaul.

During the days of enforced idleness, he had come to realize that combat flying was likely to lead to an early grave. He preferred that this grave be at Arlington National Cemetery in Virginia instead of somewhere in China, and he wanted "Gregory Boyington, U.S. Marine Corps" cut into the headstone, not "Gregory Boyington, Mercenary." Soon he was on his way to Washington, where his Chinese uniform almost got him arrested for impersonating an officer. Reinstatement in the Marine Corps came almost immediately. It was followed by a brilliant career as "Pappy" Boyington, leader of Marine Fighting Squadron 214, the Black Sheep.

In Chennault's opinion, the whole question of incorporating his volunteers into the Army Air Forces had been badly handled. General Arnold had first broached the idea shortly after Pearl Harbor, and Chennault had agreed when he conferred with Stilwell at Kunming during March. Although time for preparation had been more than adequate, no integration plan existed that took into account the war-weariness of the Flying Tigers or the fact that more than half of them, Boyington included, held commissions in the Navy or Marine Corps and had never worn the Army's silver wings. Bissell and his superiors seemed to believe that these men would give up the leave they had earned, change service affiliation if necessary and sign on for an indefinite stay in China.

The deadline for integration slipped from 30 April to 4 July, but the

B-25 raid on Japanese shipping in Hong Kong harbor

members of the American Volunteer Group were still not signing up with the Army Air Forces. When Chennault refused to make a personal appeal that his men stay on—he felt they should receive assurance that fresh squadrons would replace them as quickly as possible—Bissell addressed a meeting of the group, appealing to their patriotism and, according to Chennault, making a veiled threat to have them drafted into the Army if they returned to the United States after their contracts expired.

Whatever its contents, the speech failed to accomplish the desired effect. Only five pilots—Tex Hill, Gil Bright, Ed Rector, Frank Schiel and Charley Sawyer—and 25 ground crew members agreed to remain in China wearing the uniform of the Army Air Forces. Some individuals, principally those who felt they could no longer pass a military physical examination, stayed on to fly transports for the China National Aviation Corporation, and a few cast their lot with Pan American Airways.

A majority of the Flying Tigers left China to rejoin the services in which they held commissions. Two of them won the Medal of Honor, the nation's highest award for valor. Gregory Boyington received his for his leadership of the Black Sheep squadron in the South Pacific. Jim Howard, who rejoined the Army Air Forces, earned his medal for single-handedly breaking up an attack by German fighters on an American bomber formation.

Several of the volunteers, among them Bob Neale, John Petach, Bill

Bartling and Charley Bond, agreed to stay on temporarily and help train replacements for the departing Tigers. They intended afterward to rejoin their own services. Also remaining at Kunming was one of the group's nurses, Emma Jane Foster, who had married John Petach in February.

The American Volunteer Group flew its last missions on 4 July 1942. Several P-40s escorted a few Army Air Forces B-25s against Canton, and four of Chennault's men—Neale, Bond, Bartling and Petach—claimed six Japanese aircraft in repulsing an attack on Hengyang. In a message from Chungking, Chiang Kai-shek saluted "General Chennault and his company of air knights," while Japanese broadcasters announced the impending departure of the defeated American mercenaries.

The accomplishments of the Flying Tigers were surrounded by confusion. Lacking the gun cameras that appeared later in the war, Chennault's men had difficulty in verifying kills, for pilots fighting for their lives in kaleidoscopic aerial battles made notoriously poor witnesses. To make up for the fact that several pilots might score hits on an enemy aircraft that broke up and crashed, the volunteers quickly adopted a system of fractional credit, half-victories and even fifth-victories, but this could not compensate for enemy planes that crashed unseen, were reported independently by different eyewitnesses and counted more than once, or seemed doomed but somehow survived.

By Chennault's reckoning, the Chinese government had spent $8 million on the American Volunteer Group—$5 million to purchase the P-40Bs and other equipment, and the remainder for salaries, bonuses and expenses. He was certain that the Flying Tigers had more than justified this outlay. Statistics prepared by Olga Greenlaw credited the group with shooting down 299 enemy planes, 13 more than the total of confirmed kills paid for by the Chinese, possibly downing another 153 aircraft and destroying more than 200 on the ground. In contrast, Chennault's men lost 12 P-40s shot down in combat and 61 destroyed on the ground or in accidents. Twenty-three Flying Tigers were killed in action or as a result of accidents. Japanese losses in aerial combat with the volunteers may have totaled 1,500.

Twenty-nine men became aces, destroying five or more enemy planes in aerial fighting, while serving with the Flying Tigers. The count given is: Percy Bartlett (7.00 victories), W. E. Bartling (7.25), Lew Bishop (5.20), Charley Bond (8.75), Gregory Boyington (6.00), Gil Bright (7.00), George Burgard (10.75), Arthur Chen (5.00), Parker Dupouy (6.50), Thomas Haywood (5.25), Duke Hedman (5.00), Tex Hill (12.50), Ken Jernstedt (10.50), Chauncey Laughlin (5.20), Frank Lawlor (8.50), Robert Little (10.50), Clifford Louie (5.00), Bob Neale (15.50), Jack Newkirk (10.50), Charley Older (10.50), John Petach (5.25), Bob Prescott (5.25), Ed Rector (10.50), Bill Reed (10.50), Dick Rossi (6.25), Bob Sandell (5.25), Frank Schiel (7.00), Snuffy Smith (8.00) and Robert T. Smith (8.67).

Chinese ground warning system in action

This compilation suffers, of course, from uncertainties that arose in reconciling claims with officially credited victories. It includes victories won by members of the Flying Tigers who stayed on for a brief time after the American Volunteer Group had disbanded. In addition, some of Chennault's pilots who transferred to the Army Air Forces may have been credited as Flying Tigers for one or more victories earned as Army airmen.

Several of the Flying Tigers gained additional fame after the group had disbanded. Gregory Boyington, for example, scored 22 victories as a marine, and Jim Howard, the other Medal of Honor winner, made most of his 9.33 kills in the skies over Europe. Tex Hill added five victories in China, bringing his total to 17.50. Catfish Raines scored most of his six kills as a naval aviator, and Bill Reed claimed seven more victims while flying for Chennault after the volunteer group had disbanded.

Tex Hill, who had agreed to abandon his Navy career to remain with Chennault as a major in the Army Air Forces, acknowledged that the passing of the Flying Tigers meant more than the end of an adventure. "When you work and fight together for a long time," he said, "you hate to split up. It's like something going out of your life."

Weeks after the individual volunteers had begun drifting away from Kunming, General Arnold wrote to Chennault. "I am personally directing a major and intense effort," he said, "to enroll in the Army Air Forces all of your ex-AVG combat personnel who are now in the States." The commanding general explained that he needed the "skill, experience, and ability" that Chennault had instilled into them.

"I hope your efforts . . . will prove successful," Chennault replied, "for with hardly an exception, they are fine, dependable men, well seasoned by experience." He could not, however, resist reminding General Arnold of the haphazard way that integration of the Flying Tigers into the Army Air Forces had been handled. "If your letter had reached me in May or June," he suggested, "I am confident that a majority of the men would have enrolled here and could have been transferred to the United States in small groups over a period of several months."

Even as he offered this gentle reminder, Chennault, Hill, Petach and the others tried to recapture the spirit of the Flying Tigers and hand it on to the Army squadrons being sent to China. Replacement pilots, many of them the greenest of second lieutenants, were arriving at Kunming, new fighters and badly needed bombers appeared and a trickle of supplies crossed the Himalayas. The rebuilding had scarcely begun, and already Chennault was thinking in terms of destroying Japanese air power in China "within six months by a very modest American air force equipped with modern planes."

# 10. The Spirit of the Tigers

While General Bissell, the Tenth Air Force commander-designate was trying unsuccessfully to incorporate the Flying Tigers into the Army Air Forces, he was serving as Stilwell's air officer. He did not formally take over the Tenth Air Force until mid-July 1942, when he succeeded Brigadier General Earl Naiden, who had been temporarily in charge. Bissell's headquarters was New Delhi, India, some 2,200 miles from Kunming, where Chennault was organizing the China Air Task Force, successor to the American Volunteer Group.

Created at one minute after midnight on 5 July, the China Air Task Force was less formidable than its name would indicate. Chennault could muster just three fighter squadrons—the 74th, 75th and 76th—which formed the 23d Fighter Group under the temporary command of Bob Neale. Tex Hill assumed command of the 75th, Ed Rector took over the 76th and Frank Schiel converted the 74th into an operational training unit.

Another fighter squadron, the 16th, was sitting out the monsoon season in Assam, just beyond the Himalayas, when Chennault suggested sending it to China to gain combat experience. Tenth Air Force agreed to loan him the unit, but once he got control, he refused to release it. Among the members of the 16th Fighter Squadron was Johnny Alison, whose test

Distinguished tourists: Chennault with General Arnold (l.), General Stilwell, Field Marshal Sir John Dill, General Bissell

flight of the P-40B in the spring of 1941 had so impressed the Chinese purchasing commission.

When the 23d Fighter Group came into being, Neale's men inherited 31 P-40Bs and 20 P-40Es from the American Volunteer Group, but ground crews could put no more than 29 planes in the air on a given day. Although additional P-40Es reached the new squadrons, the buildup proceeded so slowly that Chennault had to borrow 10 Republic P-43 Lancers from the Chinese Air Force. These second-line fighters reverted to courier jobs when more P-40s became available.

During the transition period from volunteer group to air task force, while Neale commanded the fighter units, combat operations continued, with veteran Flying Tigers leading the recent arrivals on escort, interceptor and strafing missions. One of these flights claimed the life of John Petach, shot down by antiaircraft fire while bombing Japanese troops. His widow returned to her parents' home at State College, Pa. Arnold Shamblin, who also had agreed to stay on for a few weeks and help Chennault, was shot down and killed during the same mission on which Petach died. The third former Flying Tiger to die while serving in the China Air Task Force was Frank Schiel, killed in a plane crash on 8 December 1942.

Chennault's task force inherited one bombardment squadron, the 11th, which flew twin-engine North American B-25 medium bombers, the type that Doolittle's men had flown against Japan. Commanded by Major

P-40 Tomahawk in the foreground was
the first one flown by Colonel Scott

Bill Bayse, the unit encountered the same maintenance and supply problems that plagued the fighter group. For a time, only half of the B-25s were in condition for combat, and to make the situation even worse dysentery kept the squadron out of the war for an entire week. The number of airworthy B-25s gradually increased, much as the fighter group was gathering strength, so that Major Everett ("Brick") Holstrom, the veteran of Doolittle's raid who succeeded Bayse, could conduct sustained operations.

Chennault was fortunate in the officers assigned him. Colonel Robert Scott replaced Bob Neale in command of the 23d Fighter Group and occasionally functioned as the general's chief of staff. Responsible for the task force's bombardment efforts was Colonel Caleb Haynes, who had flown explosives-laden C-47s into Kunming. Besides planning missions, Haynes flew with Major Bayse's men on several raids. Before the summer had ended, however, Haynes had departed for India, where he took over the India Air Task Force.

Another of the officers sent by Bissell to Kunming was Colonel Bruce Holloway, who was assigned as task force operations officer. Upon discovering that the newcomer had no combat experience, Chennault sent him to a fighter squadron. Like the young second lieutenants fresh from training, he sat through the general's lectures on fighter tactics. Chennault later recalled that the slender native of Tennessee "had a dead-pan face" that kept the instructor from determining whether he was getting through to him. Holloway soon demonstrated, however, that he had been an alert pupil, shooting down 10 Japanese planes. The combination of combat missions and staff work so exhausted Holloway that Chennault reluctantly sent him back to the United States after a year in China. When he finally retired from the U.S. Air Force in 1972, Holloway had risen to the rank of general and commanded the Strategic Air Command, a key element in the nation's nuclear strike force.

In the summer of 1942, when he joined Chennault, Holloway received an assignment coveted by another young officer, Lieutenant Colonel Clinton D. ("Casey") Vincent. Although assigned to Bissell's headquarters, Vincent made frequent flights over the Himalayas either to conduct business at task force headquarters or to engage in combat. On 11 November 1942, for example, he led eight P-40Es to bomb and strafe "a couple of small towns occupied by Japanese soldiers and Burma sympathizers." Each pilot dropped a 500-pound bomb and six 25-pound fragmentation bombs, leaving "one large fire and numerous small fires burning." Vincent then followed a small stream until he came upon a group of Japanese soldiers disembarking from a small boat. He immediately opened fire on them, using up the last of his ammunition.

After returning to Dijan airfield in Assam, Vincent wrote down his impressions of the day's mission. "Combat flying is fun," he told his wife, "but I don't quite like this kind of fun. . . . What I'm trying to say is that while

In the alert shack—the nucleus of the 23d Fighter Group

you are in combat it is thrilling and exciting—but the aftermath, with its recollections of men running and huts burning, is not." He prayed, the letter continued, that "God forgive the part I am playing and understand why I must do it."

During the fall of 1942, Bissell decided that something had to be done to organize the administrative chaos at China Air Task Force headquarters. Chennault, after all, remained always a fighter, contemptuous of routine paperwork in his zeal for victory in the air. The Tenth Air Force commander selected Vincent to become executive officer, China Air Task Force, an appointment made without consulting Chennault.

Vincent arrived at Kunming on 12 November and, as he recounted in his diary, found the general "mad as hell about my being assigned as Executive." Once again Chennault chose to ignore Bissell's instructions, as he had when Holloway arrived, and Vincent became an operations officer helping plan missions for the 11th Bombardment Squadron.

"I don't think General Bissell is going to like it one bit when he learns I'm not being assigned to the 'Executive' job I was sent up here for," wrote Vincent in his diary. He was correct, but the change of assignment did not bother the young officer. "I am going to get some flying here," he realized, "and that's what I want."

Chennault agreed that Vincent ought to be flying. According to the general's recollection, he waited a few weeks then "advised him, 'Casey you better go out east and find out how it's done before you begin telling the other boys how to do it.' " Actually, Vincent had intended from the outset to take part in a strike against Haiphong, the first mission he had worked on after joining the task force operations section. On 22 November, he flew one of 10 bomb-carrying P-40Es that accompanied 10 B-25s over the Japanese-held port. He aimed his 500-pound bomb at a ship but missed, only to score a direct hit on a dockside warehouse.

Vincent flew five missions in the next six days. Over Canton on the 24th, he watched as the fragmentation bombs carried under the wing of a P-40 in his flight detonated, sending the plane plunging into a factory which erupted in a ball of fire. During an attack against Hong Kong on the 27th, Casey Vincent overshot one enemy fighter, which his wingman promptly destroyed, then "saw another in a turn and let go a good burst— killed the pilot and saw the plane head for the ground smoking badly." This was the first of six enemy planes that he shot down before Chennault, who at last installed him as executive officer, directed him to stay out of combat.

During his first few weeks with the China Air Task Force, Vincent frequently complained in his diary about Chennault's use of his staff and the quality of the officers assigned to it. "It's a mystery to me," the colonel wrote after one full day on the job, "how General Chennault has been able to do as much as he has with this staff." He soon discovered the answer: Chennault was his own staff, at least in matters pertaining to operations. For whatever help he needed, Chennault called on either Colonel Scott or a reserve officer, Colonel Merian C. Cooper. Although a capable planner, Scott preferred flying, something that he did exceptionally well. Before leaving China, he shot down 13 Japanese aircraft. These exploits inspired his best-selling book, *God Is My Co-Pilot*.

Much of the planning burden fell to Cooper, a World War I airman and veteran Hollywood figure, creator of the movie *King Kong*—in which Army Air Corps planes play a climactic part. Called to active duty as an air intelligence officer, Cooper was passing through Chungking en route to the Soviet Union when word reached him that he was not welcome in Russia because he had helped organize a Polish squadron to fight the Red Air Force in the turbulent months following the end of World War I.

Since he was stranded in China, Cooper obtained a staff assignment at Stilwell's headquarters. The adventurous tradition of the Flying Tigers appealed to him, however, and he talked his way into the China Air Task Force. "With his shirt tails generally flapping in the breeze, a tousled fringe of hair wreathing his bald spot, a mantle of pipe ashes over his uniform and sagging pants," wrote Chennault, "Cooper would never have passed muster at a West Point class reunion, but he was a brilliant tactician and prodigious worker." The general was delighted by what his chief of staff was doing, later declaring that "when planning a mission . . . Cooper worked round the clock until every detail was satisfactory and then rode in

Crewman overhauls the P-40 that made the first 23d Fighter

Group kill

the nose of the lead bomber, peering over the bombardier's shoulder at the target."

General Bissell, however, had never shared Chennault's enthusiasm for this sloppily dressed part-time soldier. As a result, the Tenth Air Force commander attempted to replace him, or at least neutralize his influence, by assigning to the task force experienced officers like Scott and Holloway, both of whom became involved in combat flying, and Vincent, who finally took over when Cooper returned to the United States. Fortunately, Chennault found Vincent a more than satisfactory replacement.

Bissell was justified in trying to strengthen the task force staff. Chennault, unable to recruit trained staff officers for the Flying Tigers, had become deeply involved in planning, intelligence and supply—activities that would normally be staff functions. The American Volunteer Group had operated efficiently under one-man direction, but the China Air Task Force was growing too large and its operations too complex for Chennault to handle, even with help from Cooper.

Yet, even before Bissell sought to overhaul Chennault's staff procedures, complaints had arisen about his own method of operation. Before leaving for the Middle East, General Brereton had protested to General Arnold that his harmonious relationship with General Stilwell had been disrupted by Bissell. "Prior to the arrival of General Bissell," he charged, he had experienced "no difficulty whatsoever" with Stilwell's headquarters, but after the coming of the newly appointed officer, "this happy situation started to change and steadily grew worse." Brereton said that "to be perfectly frank, he is saturated with peacetime routine and is unable to adapt himself to war conditions. For example, he calls for all sorts of detailed reports and asks far too many detailed questions that simply clutter up the communication lines to no purpose." Bissell's meticulous attitude toward paperwork could be just as infuriating as Chennault's careless approach.

After the war, Chennault echoed the charge that Bissell had become bogged down in the administrative mire, recalling in his autobiography "an exchange of terse, bitter 'eyes alone' messages between Bissell and myself." These dealt with everything from razor blades to aviation gasoline, according to Chennault, who accused his superior of failing to meet firm commitments to deliver specified amounts of cargo over the Himalayas. Bissell's devotion to bookkeeping, the task force commander complained, prevented his unit from receiving even half what had been promised it.

As the year progressed, Chennault found himself fighting a war on three fronts. He directed the China Air Task Force against the Japanese, while at the same time struggling with Bissell for the necessary supplies and battling Stilwell to obtain a greater wartime role for China-based air power. He used every means at his disposal to obtain a command independent of Bissell and Stilwell, an arrangement that he believed would enable him to carry out a plan of action that he was preparing.

Tigers look more formal as part of Army Air Forces

In August 1942 he offered Stilwell a preliminary version of this evolving concept. Chennault called for the creation of "a small, effective U.S. Air Force in China." Such a contingent would "destroy much of the war material flowing through and around Formosa. . . . Inspire Chinese ground forces to action. . . . Neutralize Jap air efforts in Burma and Indo China. Relieve the immediate Jap threat to India. Safeguard our air transport line to China, and supply a successful offensive . . ." To accomplish this, he estimated he would need "500 planes, bombers and fighters, plus 100 transports . . . plus complete authority in this theater."

Stilwell ignored the proposal. Intent upon training and arming Chinese forces for the recapture of Burma, the Army general feared the Generalissimo would seize upon Chennault's idea, so that American airmen would fight the Japanese while the Nationalist forces prepared for the eventual struggle with Mao Tse-tung and the Communists. Obviously, Stilwell could not endorse a plan that would both divert supplies from the Chinese ground forces and encourage Chiang to pull out of the planned Burma operation.

When Stilwell failed to act, Chennault executed a series of bureaucratic end runs, violations of military protocol that seemed necessary if air power was to shorten the war and save American lives. First, Merian Cooper contacted Bill Donovan, head of the Office of Strategic Services, and urged his friend to present the Chennault plan to President Roosevelt. This

**119**

Planes of the 51st Fighter Group ready for takeoff—October 1942

maneuver may have caught the attention of the Chief Executive, but it definitely angered General Arnold and speeded Cooper's departure from China.

Far more influential with Roosevelt, and immune to military discipline, was his distant cousin, Joseph Alsop, a journalist and admirer of Chennault. While an unofficial member of the Flying Tigers' staff, Alsop made a number of journeys to collect supplies needed by the American Volunteer Group, and one of these trips brought him to Hong Kong at an unfortunate time. He was there when the Crown Colony fell to the Japanese, who interned him as an enemy alien. His captors, however, later released him as part of an exchange for Japanese nationals confined in the United States.

Back in Washington, Alsop obtained an appointment as a lend-lease official in China. There he attached himself to Chennault's staff, though he did not yet hold an Army commission, and began bombarding his friends in the Roosevelt administration, especially Harry Hopkins, the President's closest aide, with arguments for the removal of Stilwell, charging among various points that the Army general underestimated the effectiveness of air power. Because the President relied heavily upon Hopkins for advice, Alsop had zeroed in on a key target.

Another important convert to Chennault's theories, besides Hopkins, was Wendell Willkie, defeated Republican presidential candidate in the

1940 election, who visited China in the fall of 1942 during a tour of world battlefronts as Roosevelt's special representative. Like most special representatives, who must try to see everything within a few days, Willkie discovered only what his Chinese hosts wanted to show him. The sight of Chiang's personal forces on parade or in carefully staged maneuvers muted the effect of Stilwell's account of his struggle to create a truly modern Chinese Army. Reform and modernization seemed unnecessary when China already had such splendid-looking troops.

Whereas Stilwell talked of improvement, which hardly seemed essential in the light of what Willkie was seeing, Chennault spoke in terms of victory, and Generalissimo and Mme. Chiang radiated confidence in the American airman. To Chennault, Willkie's visit offered an unparalleled opportunity to get out from under Stilwell and Bissell, to have first call on the cargo arriving over the Himalayas and to carry out the kind of campaign he had been planning. He drew up a concept of operation even more daring than the earlier scheme which Stilwell had ignored, incorporating it in a long memorandum that he presented to Willkie for delivery to the President.

"Japan can be defeated in China," Chennault declared; she could be beaten "by an Air Force so small that in any other theater it would be called ridiculous." This force would total only 105 fighters, 30 medium bombers and a dozen heavy bombers, plus the reserves necessary to maintain this strength. With just 147 combat planes, Chennault proposed to take advantage of Japan's "limited production of aircraft" and force the Japanese air arm "by aerial maneuver" to fight him in a position of his own selection. Having fixed it in this position, he said, "I can destroy its effectiveness." To provide fuel, munitions and other supplies for this force would require "an aerial supply line . . . between India and China," but "full establishment and maintenance of this . . . route would be child's play in comparison with the difficulties overcome in establishing the Pan American . . . . air lines."

"I am confident," Chennault continued, "that, given real command of such an Air Force, I can cause the collapse of Japan." For him, real authority meant "complete freedom of fighting action." He would be supreme American commander in China, with "authority to report only to the Generalissimo."

Willkie handed the Chennault memorandum to the President at a critical time. The Japanese were beating back a British probe of Burma, and Prime Minister Churchill was losing his enthusiasm for a full-scale invasion of the former colony, an undertaking that he compared to eating a porcupine "quill by quill." The British leader's attitude, combined with the continuing friction between Stilwell and Chiang, made Chennault's proposed aerial campaign appear to be the best means of keeping China in the war.

No amount of persuasion could have swayed Roosevelt, if the China Air Task Force had not been winning victories with its few aircraft and the small quantity of supplies that it received. The new men joining Chennault's organization had caught on quickly under the tutelage of Rector and the others, even though one group of replacement pilots proved so inexperienced that Colonel Scott had to send them back to India for further training.

One of the new arrivals was especially welcome. Out of the cabin of a C-47 stepped Ajax Baumler, now a major in the Army Air Forces, whose attempt to join the Flying Tigers had been cut short at Wake Island by the coming of war. During his service in China, Baumler would shoot down five planes, becoming one of the few Allied airmen to have destroyed aircraft bearing the insignia of all three Axis partners—Germany, Japan and Italy.

Since he was still getting his gear arranged, Baumler missed out on an attack planned against Canton for 28 July 1942. On the previous night, Japanese bombers had raided Hengyang, but swarms of Chinese laborers filled the bomb craters in time for a dawn takeoff. A formation of six bomb-laden P-40Es, commanded by Tex Hill, headed toward the target but had to turn back because of bad weather. As the frustrated strike force was returning to Hengyang, ground observers reported 70 enemy fighters approaching the airfield. Low on fuel, besides being outnumbered, the P-40s could not possibly fight their way through to land. Hill realized, however, that the Japanese always monitored American radio channels, so he began issuing orders to nonexistent squadrons. His men quickly caught onto his scheme, and soon the air was alive with chatter. Convinced they were outnumbered, the enemy doubled back to Hankow.

On the following evening, Baumler, Hill and Johnny Alison went aloft to intercept a flight of bombers that the warning net had reported bound for the Hengyang airdrome. The three men kept low in order to spot the exhaust plumes beneath the enemy's engines. These tactics succeeded, and Alison led the way toward the raiders, which now were turning to begin their bomb runs. Eager for a kill, he climbed too rapidly and leveled off a few hundred feet above his intended victim, enabling the tail gunner to spot him against the sky. The Japanese opened fire at close range, blasting a hole in the P-40's engine. But Alison kept boring in, setting fire to this bomber, then detonating the explosives stowed inside the fuselage of a second plane.

While Baumler was claiming two kills of his own, Alison attempted to land his damaged fighter, but oil leaking from the engine caught fire. His fellow pilots on the ground could see his plane streak past like a comet, overshooting the runway and disappearing in the direction of a nearby river. When he landed and discovered that Alison was missing, Tex Hill vowed to avenge the loss.

On the following morning, while leading 10 P-40s against a flight of 35 Nakajima Ki 43s, Hill had his opportunity for revenge. He singled out the Japanese leader and, covered by his wingman, went head-on after the enemy. The greater American firepower overwhelmed the lighter plane, which nosed over, trailing smoke, as Hill's fighter screamed past. The Nakajima exploded among some dummy P-40s that had been built near the airfield as decoys.

Hill's act of vengeance, it turned out, was unnecessary. Miraculously, Alison had brought his burning plane down on the river east of the runway. Some Chinese rescued him from the water and took him to a Roman Catholic mission, where the priest bandaged his head, badly cut when Japanese bullets had shattered the windscreen of his P-40. Within 48 hours, Alison was safely back at Hengyang.

The new Ki 43s, the type that Hill had outgunned in his head-on attack, proved to be a formidable aircraft. Chennault later acknowledged that "in the hands of an experienced pilot, the Oscar"—as the plane was labeled by the Allies—"could fly rings around the P-40." Designed in 1938 by Hideo Itokawa, the prototype had proved woefully sluggish, compared with the agile Ki 27. Itokawa had corrected this weakness by increasing the wing area and installing the so-called battle flap, which the pilot could extend during combat to improve the plane's responsiveness. The first models encountered by the China Air Task Force mounted just two heavy

Tigers' base at Kweilin is well protected by nature

machine guns, but some advanced versions boasted a pair of 20-mm cannon plus armor and a crude type of self-sealing fuel tank.

Despite opposition from these fighters and from improved models of the Zero, Chennault's fliers conducted frequent raids against the port of Canton and its satellite airfields, using both B-25s and P-40Es. The strike force usually flew over a salient held by Chinese troops, so that the defenders had only about five minutes' warning. As the Japanese climbed to intercept, the escorting P-40s tried to dive on them out of the sun. Success over Canton emboldened Chennault to decide to attack Hong Kong.

On 24 October the general assembled a force of 10 P-40s and a dozen B-25s at the Kweilin airfield in eastern China. Some of the bombers had flown all the way from India, led by Colonel Caleb Haynes, who was determined to take part in this first American attack on the Japanese-held Crown Colony. Once again Tex Hill led the fighter cover. The strike, delivered on the morning of the 25th, caught the enemy by surprise. Haynes's force dumped several tons of Russian-built demolition bombs, the same as those dropped from P-40Es on the Salween River bridge site, on ships moored along the Kowloon peninsula. Unfortunately, the American bombardiers had no previous experience with these weapons, which behaved differently from the standard 500-pounders they normally used, so that most of the explosives detonated among waterfront shacks and warehouses. Many of the casualties were Chinese dock workers, though some military cargo was destroyed.

Japanese interceptors were taking off by the time the bombs began falling. Hill's pilots employed the tactics that had worked so well over Canton, diving with the sun at their backs—"like a flock of vultures spotting carrion," Chennault would write—and shooting down most of the 20 enemy planes destroyed that day. One India-based B-25 suffered mortal damage as it headed inland from the target, but the pilot managed a successful crash landing. Japanese troops captured four crewmen, but two others made their way to Chinese lines. One P-40 also went down during this first Hong Kong raid.

The 11 surviving B-25s landed at Kweilin, where nine of them refueled and took on bombs and ammunition. Shortly after midnight, Major Bill Bayse led six of the planes against the Hong Kong electric power plant, while three other bombers raided Canton. All the planes returned safely.

During the months that followed, the China Air Task Force divided its efforts between northern Burma and eastern China, with an occasional foray into Indochina. Chennault grumbled when Bissell asked him to ease pressure on the aerial supply route by bombing fighter bases at Lashio and Myitkyina in Burma, but he complied, though he later complained that the missions had been a waste of precious gasoline. Attacks against targets in Burma usually originated at Kunming or Yunnanyi. Hengyang served as the base for strikes against Canton or in the Hankow region, and raids against Canton, Hong Kong or places in Indochina continued to stage through Kweilin.

At the end of November, Chennault's men put on a dazzling display, hitting the enemy from different airfields and demonstrating how their commander hoped to make the Japanese fight on his terms. On 23 November, P-40s from Kweilin lashed at Indochina, hitting the ports of Hon Gay and Haiphong, plus coastal shipping. On the following day, the B-25s joined in, raiding airfields near Canton. One enemy base, on Sauchau Island, was devoid of planes, but intelligence specialists estimated that 42 Japanese aircraft were destroyed or damaged at Tien Ho. The nearby port of Whampoa came under attack on the 25th.

To divert attention from the Canton area and northern Indochina, Chennault dispatched B-25s against Hankow and neighboring towns. He protected Hengyang airfield, through which the bombers staged, by sending five P-40s on an unexpected night mission against Hankow. The fighters took off from Hengyang, hit the airfield and docks with 500-pound bombs and returned safely.

The China Air Task Force next massed at Kweilin. After his staff officers had planted a rumor that Hong Kong was the next target, Chennault launched his aircraft against Canton. On 27 November, the B-25s claimed the destruction of two ships and two to four Japanese fighters while bombing the waterfront. The 21 escorting P-40s reported 22 kills, most of them Ki 43s, and four probables. Two damaged American fighters made emergency landings in friendly territory, though short of Kweilin.

Hong Kong harbor was recurring target for the Americans

This six-day flurry of activity ended on 28 November with attacks upon shipping in the Gulf of Tonkin. The China Air Task Force had flown 11 missions in rapid succession, hitting targets as much as 800 miles apart and reporting the destruction of three ships and 71 planes, together with damage to port and airfield facilities. Although the estimated damage, like all such reports, was subject to challenge, the series of raids lent credence to Chennault's claim that he could defeat Japan through air power.

Early in 1943, President Roosevelt decided to carry out the kind of aerial campaign described in the memorandum that Wendell Willkie had brought back from China. Emphasizing air power would mollify Chiang and also reassure Churchill that resources needed in Europe were not being squandered on the Asian mainland. Typically, the President tried to compromise, leaving Stilwell as overall American commander but making Chennault the equal of Bissell. As a result, on 3 March 1943 Major General Claire L. Chennault pinned on a second star, and one week later he assumed command of the China-based Fourteenth Air Force.

With the creation of the Fourteenth Air Force, Chennault could look back with pride on the accomplishments of the China Air Task Force during its eight months of existence. In his autobiography, he declared, "The China Air Task Force was probably the smallest American Air Force ever to be dignified by the command of a general. It certainly was the raggedest. Its paper work was poor, and salutes were scarce, but when the sig-

Generalissimo and Mme. Chiang Kai-shek at his 1943 inauguration

nals were called for combat, it never missed a play." By his count, the task force had shot down 149 planes in aerial combat and possibly downed another 85, all at the cost of 16 P-40s and one B-25. His bombers had dropped 314 tons of bombs—which he admitted was "less than one quarter of the weight of a single Eighth Air Force mission over Germany"—but he insisted that this tonnage had "shattered the security of the Japanese in their vast base on the Asiatic mainland."

When the Fourteenth Air Force came into being, Chennault himself was its principal link with Flying Tiger days. John Petach, Frank Schiel and Arnold Shamblin had died in China since the American Volunteer Group had disbanded. Tex Hill, Ed Rector, Gil Bright and Charley Sawyer had left for the United States, though Hill and Rector would return, as would George McMillan, another of the original Flying Tigers. Bob Neale, along with the others who had agreed to remain behind for a short while and had survived the time of transition, had said farewell by the end of July. For the time being, the spirit of the American Volunteer Group was embodied in Chennault. The only other links with the past were Dr. Tom Gentry, a flight surgeon for the Tigers who had stayed on as the general's personal physician; Joe Alsop, who still awaited his commission in the Army Air Forces; and Ajax Baumler, recruited for the original group, though he had been unable to join it.

Could the Fourteenth Air Force live up to Flying Tiger traditions and accomplish all that Chennault claimed it could? Did the series of strikes late in November really demonstrate the versatility of air power and the soundness of the general's plan? Did the small tonnage of bombs dropped by the China Air Task Force B-25s prove that the Japanese could easily be hurt or merely underscore the difficulty of delivering larger quantities of munitions over the mountains to the units based in China? The next few months would provide the answers.

# 11. Confirming the Chennault Plan

Before Chennault could launch his air campaign in China, Allied political and military leaders had to fit the undertaking into their overall strategy and make sure that logistical preparations were adequate. By creating the Fourteenth Air Force, President Roosevelt had shown his determination to stress air power in China. This action, however, did not fix Allied strategy in the Far East; as usual, worldwide military priorities had to be hammered out at one of the periodic conferences where Allied leaders planned the defeat of the Axis powers. The next meeting in this series, code-named Trident, was scheduled for Washington in May 1943. Prime Minister Churchill, who had begun questioning the wisdom of attacking Japanese forces in Burma, would of course be present, and the President therefore wanted to have an agreed American strategy that could be presented during Trident.

Chiang Kai-shek, who championed the Chennault plan of fighting the Japanese mainly in the air, persuaded Roosevelt to summon Chennault to Washington for consultations on the eve of the Trident conference. When General George C. Marshall, the U.S. Army Chief of Staff, asked Stilwell about the President's planned meeting with Chennault, the theater commander replied that he knew nothing about it. Marshall then told the President, "To call in Chennault and ignore Stilwell . . . would create such a division of authority . . . as to necessitate Stilwell's relief and Chennault's appointment to command of ground and air, which as far as I am concerned would be a grave mistake." Since the President had retained Stilwell in overall command when he placed Chennault in charge of the Fourteenth Air Force, he proved receptive to Marshall's advice, summoning both generals to Washington. During the final preparations for Trident, the two men presented their conflicting ideas for waging war on the Asian mainland.

While a military transport plane was bringing Stilwell and Chennault to the capital, T. V. Soong delivered a note from the Generalissimo to President Roosevelt. In it Chiang urged adoption of the Chennault plan, claiming that the ground war need not be "sacrificed" in order to supply the Fourteenth Air Force. "It will be understood," said the Nationalist leader, "that after the required reserves for the air offensive have been accumulated, the percentage of the air tonnage into China allocated to aviation supplies can be reduced to the total needed merely to maintain the air effort." As the capacity of the aerial route expanded, he predicted, "all needed ground supplies may also be carried into China in ample time to be on hand when needed." Probably the most important part of Chiang's letter was his "personal assurance" that in the event the enemy attempted to interrupt the air offensive by a ground advance on the air bases, the advance could be halted by the existing Chinese forces.

Scarcely had Chennault left for Washington when the Japanese bombed Yunnanyi airdrome, killing more than 200 Chinese laborers working on the runways and two Americans. The raid destroyed five P-40s and a C-47 and damaged 11 fighters. For several days enemy bombers had approached the airfield, turning back as soon as the American fighters became airborne. Because they were short of gasoline, the defenders became concerned about burning up their remaining fuel while responding to feints. As a result, the officer responsible for protecting Yunnanyi waited until the last possible moment before committing his fighters, but on this particular day the innermost station in the warning net lost contact with the airfield, permitting the enemy to achieve complete surprise.

When the two generals reached Washington, the day was 29 April in the Orient, Emperor Hirohito's birthday. As usual, the Japanese tried to win an aerial victory in his honor, and this time they succeeded. Enemy bombers slipped past the defending fighters and struck Kunming, demolishing the base motor pool, killing two American officers, and wounding Brigadier General Edgar E. ("Buzz") Glenn, Chennault's recently arrived second in command.

During the long flight across Africa and over the Atlantic, Chennault put the final touches on a revised version of his plan, typed by Joseph Alsop before the general left China. Over a period of three days, 30 April

General George C. Marshall

Chennault's plan called for 48 B-25s like this one

through 2 May, President Roosevelt talked with both Chennault and Stilwell. The airman led off, presenting his latest estimate of the number of aircraft he would need; it totaled 233 combat planes—75 P-40s, 75 P-51s, 48 B-25s and 35 B-24s, plus reconnaissance craft—instead of the original 147. Operations would commence in July, when the weather improved in eastern China. His first objective would be attrition of the enemy air force through fighter sweeps, supported by strafing attacks and B-25 raids on airfields. Beginning in September, these medium bombers would attack shipping in the Formosa Strait and South China Sea, while the B-24 Liberators hit Shanghai, Nanking and the island of Formosa. By the end of November, Fourteenth Air Force would be sinking enemy ships from Pusan in Korea to Cam Ranh Bay in Indochina and dispatching the Liberator bombers to hammer cities on the Japanese Home Islands of Honshu and Kyushu. To sustain this offensive, Chennault would need 4,790 tons of supplies per month from July through September. Afterward the monthly total would have to average 7,129 tons.

In conversations with General Marshall and Secretary of War Henry L. Stimson, Chennault elaborated on his plan. He believed that his men could disrupt river traffic, forcing the enemy to surrender control of the Yangtze Valley, though Japan would still hold the mainland ports and the island of Formosa. In addition, air power would sink a half-million tons of shipping in just six months, while destroying Japanese aerial strength in China.

Chennault plan foresaw large-scale B-24 raids

Stilwell had no faith in Chennault's plan of action, although he conceded that with the proposed aerial striking force "the Japs could be done considerable injury." He reminded General Marshall that the Doolittle raid had triggered immediate retaliation. "Just one point about the whole thing," he said, "and that is, as we found out last spring, any attempt to bomb Japan is going to bring prompt and violent reaction on the ground, and somebody has to decide how far we can sting them before that reaction appears." If hurt badly enough, he suggested, "they may decide it would be advantageous for them to take Chungking and Kunming. If that is done, we will have to fold out there."

In Stilwell's opinion, success in China depended not on air power to hit the Japanese but on ground forces to stop the enemy when he reacted to these blows. "If we are going to bomb Japan," he told Marshall, "we will have to have China bases. I see no way except by development of a ground force. The solution is to build up the Chinese Army to a point where they can do the job."

When he talked with the President, Stilwell outlined his objections to emphasizing air power at the expense of ground forces. He criticized the Chinese for neglecting "their obligation of furnishing the manpower" which the Americans were to equip and train and for stressing "the desirability of confining activity in China to the air area." He failed, however, to convince Roosevelt.

Stilwell's failure resulted in part from his personality. He hated to push himself and apparently felt that in trying to sell his program he was arguing his own importance. Besides, he could only talk about what could not be done, while Chennault proposed going on the offensive almost immediately. Stilwell warned that Chiang could not be trusted and that extensive training would have to precede a Chinese ground operation. In contrast, Chennault told the President that the Generalissimo was "one of the two or three greatest military and political leaders in the world" and that the Fourteenth Air Force, if it received 10,000 tons of supplies each month, could sink a million tons of enemy shipping in a year. As Chennault recalled the conversation, the President, delighted by this assurance, "banged his fist on the desk and chortled, 'If you can sink a million tons, we'll break their back.'" Roosevelt, in fact, was so impressed that he encouraged the airman to report directly to him, bypassing both Stilwell and Arnold.

Nor could the Joint Chiefs of Staff agree on the comparative merits of the Stilwell and Chennault approaches. One of the most influential of their number, Admiral William D. Leahy, Chief of Staff to the President, backed Chennault, while the other service chiefs inclined toward Stilwell. Even General Arnold, though a firm believer in strategic bombing, questioned the soundness of the air offensive that Chennault recommended.

Arnold's doubts resulted from his visit to China following the conference of Allied leaders at Casablanca in January 1943. He had met Chiang Kai-shek, whose views seemed to him totally unrealistic. In his autobiography, *Global Mission*, the Commanding General, Army Air Forces, complained that the Generalissimo "brushed too many important things aside," including "logistics and factual matters," which he dismissed as "mere trifles." Chiang's "only thought" appeared to be "Aid to China! Aid to China!" The Chinese leader insisted that determination alone could accomplish the impossible. Although Arnold agreed that this quality was important, he knew that willpower could not replace gasoline in the tanks of China-based bombers. Indeed, when Chennault outlined his plans for General Marshall and the other members of the Joint Chiefs of Staff, Arnold became concerned by the "oversimplification, along Chinese lines, of various problems . . ."

Though disturbed that Chennault might have been influenced by the Generalissimo's reasoning, Arnold was shocked by Stilwell's loathing for the Chinese commander in chief. While assigned as Chiang's principal military assistant, the Army general called his nominal chief "Peanut," characterizing him as both incompetent and dishonest. Arnold, however, did not attribute Stilwell's remarks to contempt for an alien people, for he believed the American officer was lashing out at the person thought to be responsible for the corruption and mismanagement that was impeding China's war effort.

Granted that Stilwell's attitude might be self-defeating, raising ob-

General Arnold (r.) with Colonel Jacob Smart on China trip

stacles to his efforts to prod the Chinese into ground combat against the enemy, Arnold became convinced that Chennault's enthusiasm was equally mistaken. The single-minded airman appeared to be ignoring vital questions of Chinese morale and efficiency, not to mention logistics, in his zeal to get on with the war. Arnold feared that Chennault was postponing these problems instead of trying to address them.

The heart condition that eventually killed him prevented Arnold from taking part in the formal sessions of the Trident conference. During these meetings, Churchill proposed bypassing Burma to attack the oil-rich Netherlands East Indies, but Roosevelt argued that such an undertaking would be a diversion of effort, a detour from the direct route toward Japan. Concerned that China might collapse, the President insisted upon taking the offensive there immediately, a course of action that only the Chennault plan would permit. The Anglo-American Combined Chiefs of Staff tried to resolve three conflicting proposals: the British suggestion to bypass Burma; the U.S. War Department's plan to reorganize, train and equip Chinese armies for the recapture of Burma; and President Roosevelt's project to launch an air offensive in China.

Out of the conference came compromise. Stilwell would include newly trained Chinese forces in an attempt to seize northern Burma, and Chennault would receive, beginning in fall 1943, the bulk of the 10,000 tons of cargo delivered each month, so his Fourteenth Air Force could intensi-

Fourteenth Air Force adopts its Flying Tiger emblem

fy operations in China. The British obtained this curtailment of the Burma campaign, originally envisioned as an advance all the way to Rangoon, instead of the desired offensive against the Netherlands East Indies.

The subject of military operations in the China-Burma-India Theater arose again at the Quadrant conference, held at Quebec in August 1943. The conferees, in effect, ratified the Trident strategy, agreeing to double the volume of supplies delivered each month to China and scheduling the attack into northern Burma for the autumn of that year. The Allied leaders also directed their planning staffs to consider an Army Air Forces proposal to establish the new B-29 very-long-range bombers at bases in China, from which they would conduct the strategic bombardment of Japan. The huge planes, requiring their own logistical support, would remain independent of the Fourteenth Air Force.

At Quebec, Arnold made a decision that deprived Chennault of a valued subordinate. During the meetings Orde Wingate, a British brigadier, told Arnold of a plan for airborne operations deep in Japanese-held Burma. The Commanding General, Army Air Forces, was so impressed that he agreed to assign two of his best colonels to Wingate's venture. One of them was Johnny Alison, a mainstay of the China Air Task Force.

Deciding to build up the Fourteenth Air Force and unleash it against the Japanese, as had been done at Trident and confirmed at Quadrant, was simple enough; sending it the necessary fuel, munitions and other supplies proved infinitely more difficult. Part of the problem was finding a suitable transport, for the workhorse C-47 performed badly at high altitude. A bigger, more powerful plane was needed to fly the Himalayas.

A cargo version of the Consolidated B-24 Liberator, the C-87, offered a possible alternative. The four-engine plane had range and cargo capacity that seemed ideal for flying the "Hump," as the route across the mountains was called, but the transport model did not perform as well as the bomber from which it had been derived. Pilots like Ernest K. Gann, the aviator and novelist, complained that the C-87 was a truly vicious airplane, with wings that could ice up in a matter of seconds, destroying lift and tipping the huge craft into a spin. Controls were sluggish, especially at low altitude where the air was dense; the cabin heater seemed to have just two settings, freezing and broiling; instrument-panel lighting, when it worked, was so bright that pilot and copilot could not see beyond the windscreen into the night. At high altitude, the electric controls that adjusted propeller pitch tended to freeze, and whenever the crew transferred fuel from the reserve tanks, gasoline fumes collected throughout the boxlike fuselage, turning the craft into a flying bomb. During takeoffs the C-87 seemed to roll forever before thundering reluctantly into the air, a nasty trait that once almost killed Gann and the members of his crew. Before taking off from Agra, India, he underestimated the weight of the fuel on board and barely cleared the Taj Mahal as he coaxed his overloaded cargo plane into the sky.

The basic C-87 was bad, but the tanker version was even worse. Modified to carry high-octane gasoline over the Hump to Chennault's squadrons, the Liberator tanker, called the C-109, resembled a plumber's nightmare. A pinhole leak in a pipe or storage tank, a spark—and the plane exploded, vanishing without a trace. As a result, pilots took to calling the craft the "C-one-oh-boom."

For flying the route across the Hump, General Arnold relied heavily upon the Curtiss C-46 Commando. This large twin-engine transport had been designed in 1936 under the supervision of George Page, chief engineer at the Curtiss-Wright factory in St. Louis. Page intended his plane to compete with the smaller Douglas DC-3. A civilian prototype of the Page design, powered by two 1,500 horsepower Wright Cyclone engines, flew for the first time in the spring of 1940, too late for peacetime service with domestic air lines.

At the time, General Arnold was looking for a transport larger than the DC-3 and with greater range. He placed orders for both the four-engine Douglas DC-4, known as the C-54, and the C-46, so that his service would have at least one satisfactory plane. Fitted with 2,000-horsepower engines, the C-46 entered service between India and China in the spring of 1943, crossing a range of mountains 100 miles wide with peaks in excess of 24,000 feet. Along the route from Dinjan in Assam to Kunming, nicknamed the "Aluminum Trail" because of the crashed planes that littered its almost 500 miles, the Curtiss Commando cruised at about 180 miles per hour, maintaining an altitude of 20,000 to 22,000 feet and carrying 10 tons of cargo in its dolphin-shaped fuselage.

Enthusiasts for the C-46 applauded the use of just two of the most powerful engines available (rather than four smaller engines), claiming that this choice simplified maintenance. Pilots remained skeptical, however, since the loss of one engine deprived the heavily loaded airplane of half its power. Their description of the Commando as "the world's only two-engine four-engine plane" was not meant to be flattering.

Events soon demonstrated that crew members had a number of problems to complain about. Rushed into a demanding kind of service, the C-46 developed some severe teething troubles. The loss rate, as high as one plane for every 218 flights, caused General Arnold to ask Curtiss-Wright for assistance, and the company responded with a four-man engineering task force headed by Herb Fisher. These men discovered, among various difficulties, that the rubber used for fuel-line connections deteriorated in the extreme cold, allowing gasoline to leak onto hot engines and ignite. Besides correcting this problem, the team also found that the sun beating down upon aircraft parked in Assam heated the gasoline in the tanks, forming air bubbles that were pumped into the engines, causing them to mis-

Curtiss C-46 Commando flies the Hump

fire. Fisher himself made 96 flights over the Hump before satisfying himself that he had learned all the plane's foibles and remedied those that could be corrected. In some cases, however, all the team members could do was warn pilots to change procedures to compensate for persisting problems. Fisher discovered, for instance, that during night takeoffs pilots tended to reduce power too soon, probably because of momentary disorientation. He therefore insisted that they concentrate on the instruments, holding the air speed at 130 miles per hour until reaching an altitude of 300 feet.

In June 1943, after the Trident conference had approved an intensified air war in China, the India-China Wing of the U.S. Air Transport Command had 46 of these C-46s, a dozen C-87s and 80-odd C-47s. With this force, Colonel Edward Alexander managed to deliver a monthly total of 2,382 tons, barely half enough for the Fourteenth Air Force, let alone for both Chennault's command and the Chinese armed forces. Despite problems with the C-46, accidents and attacks by Japanese fighters from Burma, Alexander and his successor, Brigadier General Earl S. Hoag, managed to build up the organization and by the end of the year surpass the goal of 10,000 tons per month established during Trident.

To increase the tonnage reaching China, the wing paid a high price in human life. Between June and December 1943, 168 crew members died trying to fly the Hump. In an effort to reduce this toll, the organization set up a rescue unit, commanded by Captain John F. ("Blackie") Porter, which used C-47s to search for downed airmen, dropped medical assistance to them and arranged for rescue parties to lead them to safety. Lieutenant Colonel Don Flickinger, a flight surgeon, led some of the medical teams that parachuted into the wilderness. One of the individuals brought through the jungle was a young war correspondent, Eric Sevareid, later to be the eminent television commentator. In spite of the heroic efforts of men like Porter and Flickinger, the total number of airmen killed remained high, but the figures were misleading, because of the increase in aerial activity over the Hump. A more accurate index was the number of deaths per 1,000 flying hours, which declined from 1.9 early in 1944 to .5 a year later.

Obviously, the India-China Wing needed more and bigger aircraft to push the monthly tonnage still higher. By the spring of 1945, roughly 40 C-54s, 190 C-46s and 90 C-87s or C-109s were available for flights over the Hump. As a result, the organization's new commanders, Brigadier Generals Thomas O. Hardin and William H. Tunner, shattered the earlier records. On a single day in 1944, for example, the wing carried 15,845 tons of cargo into China.

More than military supplies crossed the Himalayas, unfortunately. At one time, Army investigators were looking into 300 cases involving the smuggling of everything from black-market cigarettes to prostitutes. Stilwell, infuriated that commissioned officers would behave in such a fashion, blamed Chennault for failing to prevent their criminal activity. Those who had bemoaned Chinese ethics might well have noted that Oriental peoples did not have a monopoly on corruption.

Although deliveries by the aerial route over the Hump surpassed the original goals, the demand for supplies steadily increased. The Allies adopted General Arnold's plan to base B-29s in China, a decision that created a need for additional tons of fuel and other cargo. Moreover, a Japanese offensive compelled the Chinese Army to expend large amounts of munitions and supplies. Partially offsetting these burdens was an improvement in the distribution of supplies throughout northern Burma. In August 1944, Stilwell's ground forces captured Myitkyina, which became the terminus of a highway and pipeline as well as an aerial supply depot.

During World War II, the Hump operation delivered an estimated 650,000 tons of cargo to China. Had ports been available, only 70 cargo ships could have disgorged this same amount, but the Japanese controlled every harbor from northeastern China to Burma. Without this massive airlift, Chennault would never have been able to launch the air offensive approved in May 1943 at the Trident conference.

# 12. Chennault's Air Offensive

The tempo of the air war picked up even as Chennault was explaining his plan to General Marshall, Secretary Stimson and President Roosevelt. Despite the successful Japanese attacks upon Yunnanyi and Kunming, the 23d Fighter Group inflicted severe losses on the enemy during April and early May. Captain John Hampshire, for instance, shot down 14 aircraft, most of them Ki 43s, in just six aerial battles. He scored his last two victories on 2 May 1943, downing a pair of the Nakajima fighters before a round fired from this same type of plane penetrated the cockpit of his P-40 and buried itself in his stomach. Hampshire managed to crash-land in the Siang River near Changsha. Chinese civilians dragged him unconscious from the wreckage, but before they could take him to the nearest hospital, he had bled to death.

A key element in Chennault's proposed air offensive, the 308th Bombardment Group, began arriving in China during May. Colonel Eugene Beebe, a former aide to General Arnold, commanded the group, which flew glass-nosed B-24Ds until B-24Js reached the unit in 1944. A power-operated gun turret added to the latter model altered the shape of the nose and provided space to paint sharks' teeth, a symbol the Fourteenth Air Force had borrowed from the China Air Task Force, which had in turn inherited it from the Flying Tigers.

Besides leading the 308th, an assignment he held until the late summer of 1943 when Arnold transferred him to India, Beebe served as the eyes of his commanding general. Throughout his service in the Far East, Beebe exchanged letters with Arnold. Although this arrangement was irregular, the chief of Army Air Forces apparently felt that he needed an observer to help him sift through the charges and countercharges being exchanged by Chennault and Stilwell. Following the establishment of the Fourteenth Air Force, the quarreling became so intense that Casey Vincent, acting at the time as Chennault's chief of staff, confessed that he was "goddamn sick of this dull political war" between the two generals.

Although Chennault expected to use the B-24s against Formosa, North China and ultimately Japan, Casey Vincent proved less than enthusiastic about the four-engine bombers. "Seems we are getting something we don't want," he wrote in his diary when he heard that Beebe's group was coming. Vincent's attitude was to some extent justified; in spite of their striking power—they could carry four tons of bombs—the planes burned as much as one gallon of high-test gasoline for each mile they flew. Every drop of this fuel had to be flown over the Hump.

Beebe's Liberators brought bombs and drums of fuel with them when they flew from India into China. As a result, he had 18 B-24Ds ready for

B-24 makes a sloshy takeoff

Liberator starts for home after bombing Vinh, Indochina

action as early as 2 May. These Liberators joined 12 B-25s and 18 P-40s in a complex mission that struck two targets almost 200 miles apart. The entire force flew to Lao Kay, just south of the border between China and Indochina, then headed southwest along the Red River to Hanoi, where the raiders divided into two groups. The medium bombers and fighters continued to the nearby port of Haiphong, while the B-24s shaped a course for Samah Bay at the southern end of Hainan Island. Although cloud cover prevented the B-25s from attacking their primary target, a cement plant, nine of the planes bombed the harbor, setting at least one large fire. The Liberators, after crossing the Tonkin Gulf, struck an airfield, docks, an oil refinery with its tank farm and a coal storage area. One plane was lost that day, a B-24 that experienced mechanical difficulty during the return flight, but all except one crew member escaped by parachute.

Beebe's group made frequent flights to India to replenish its stocks of bombs, fuel and ammunition, since the Hump airlift had just begun gathering momentum. During combat operations, aerial gunners on board the Liberators claimed the destruction of large numbers of enemy fighters. After a 31 May strike on Ichang, for example, gunners reported they had definitely shot down 20 Japanese interceptors and possibly destroyed five others. A dozen of Beebe's planes took part in a 21 August raid on Hankow, which generated claims of 57 Japanese downed in a 30-minute battle at the cost of two B-24s lost and 10 damaged. During the bomb run, Major Tosho

Sakagawa, flying a Ki 43, attacked the lead bomber head-on, shooting it down, but he could not prevent the others from boring in to destroy a fuel dump and score a direct hit on a naval headquarters. The second Liberator lost that day sustained heavy damage as it left Hankow but crash-landed in friendly territory with three dead and two wounded men on board.

Chinese Army intelligence, which reported the results of the bombing, could not find wreckage to verify anything like the number of kills claimed by Beebe's gunners. Crew members had been unable to isolate individual victims, with several men reporting the same fighter as destroyed. Also, a worn Japanese engine burning oil resembled an engine on fire, so many a supposed victim of the .50-caliber guns emerged without a scratch.

Hankow proved a costly target. Just three days later, half of a 14-plane heavy bomber force had to turn back short of the city because of bad weather. Some 40 Ki 43s fought their way through the 14 P-40s and eight P-38s serving as an escort, ignored a half-dozen B-25s and concentrated on the remaining Liberators, shooting down four of the big planes and damaging the other three. The Japanese lost three fighters in winning this aerial victory.

The twin-engine, twin-boom Lockheed P-38 Lightnings that helped escort this mission to Hankow belonged to the 449th Fighter Squadron, which had recently joined the 23d Fighter Group. In addition, the group received the latest model P-40K, M and N Warhawks. Later in 1943, the 51st Fighter Group joined Chennault's air force, with three squadrons of new P-40s and one of P-38s. The 33d and 81st Fighter Groups, totaling six squadrons of Republic P-47s, arrived during 1944, as did the 311th Fighter Group, consisting of three squadrons of North American P-51s, and a separate squadron of twin-engine Northrop P-61 Black Widow night fighters. Rounding out the Fourteenth Air Force were a photoreconnaissance squadron, equipped with modified P-38s, that entered service in the summer of 1943, two C-47 squadrons that arrived in 1944 and two additional B-25 squadrons that undertook their first missions in January 1944. Beginning in the fall of 1944, P-51 Mustangs replaced the P-40 Warhawks throughout Chennault's command.

As a result of these changes, Fourteenth Air Force fighter pilots flew three excellent aircraft, all of them superior to the best of the P-40 series, during the latter months of the war. Designed by Alexander Kartveli, the barrel-chested P-47 Thunderbolt, with its 2,000-horsepower radial engine, mounted eight .50-caliber machine guns. Kelly Johnson's P-38, powered by two supercharged Allison engines, had a 20-mm cannon and four .50-caliber machine guns firing from its nose. Different models of the P-51 served in China. The Allison-powered versions remained exclusively low-altitude fighters, but those driven by Packard-built copies of the Rolls-Royce Merlin engine could tear an enemy apart with their six .50-caliber guns at altitudes up to 25,000 feet. The Mustang's designers—Raymond

Rice, Edgar Schmued and Edward Horkey—had pooled their talents to devise an aerodynamically clean aircraft featuring an airfoil that created powerful lift with a minimum of drag. Their product, with its laminar flow wing, proved as deadly as it was handsome.

The Japanese had kept pace, however, introducing several improved fighters, among them the Kawasaki Ki 61. Just as the Mustang used an American version of the British Merlin, Kawasaki's designers planned their aircraft around a German Daimler-Benz engine built under license in Japan. Since Takeo Doi, Kawasaki's chief of design, and his assistants had studied in Germany, their sleek product resembled a Messerschmitt Me 109, for which it was sometimes mistaken. Though slightly slower than its American contemporaries, the Ki 61 could outmaneuver them, and its two 20-mm cannon and two machine guns provided adequate firepower.

When Tex Hill returned to China in the fall of 1943 after a brief tour as an instructor in the United States, these changes had already begun. He found that Chennault's command was increasing in both numbers and striking power. No longer did a few dozen P-40Bs, almost obsolete and barely airworthy, try to defend China's cities against waves of Japanese bombers.

A new group of pilots, flying these modern fighters, soon established records that rivaled the victory totals run up by their predecessors in the

Fourteenth Air Force guide to Hankow

"Pappy" Herbst with his North American P-51

Flying Tigers and China Air Task Force. Lieutenant Colonel John C. ("Pappy") Herbst, a gray-haired 36-year-old veteran, received credit for 15 aerial victories while commanding the 74th Fighter Squadron, Frank Schiel's old unit. John Hampshire would probably have surpassed Herbst's total had death not intervened. As successful as Hampshire in scoring aerial victories was Lieutenant Colonel Edward O. McComas, also with 14 triumphs, while Major James England had 10 kills. Like Tex Hill, Charley Older continued his victory string after the Flying Tigers disbanded, eventually shooting down 18.50 victims. Another veteran, Colonel Robert Scott, returned to China too late to add to his total.

Perhaps the most unusual record amassed during the China fighting was that run up by Major Thomas A. Reynolds, who destroyed 41.50 Japanese planes, three of them in aerial combat but all the rest on the ground. He served with the Chinese-American Composite Wing, consisting of one bomber and two fighter groups, an organization manned by Chinese airmen trained in the United States, though American officers held staff and combat positions. Bill Reed, a former Flying Tiger, scored several kills while a member of this force.

In his leading of men like McComas, Reynolds, and Reed, General Chennault continued to display the same ingenuity he had shown in directing the Flying Tigers. For instance, when Japanese fighters based in Burma began attacking C-87s flying the Hump, he had Colonel Bill Fisher, Beebe's replacement, send armed B-24s over the route. When the enemy mistook the bombers for Liberator transports and attacked, American gunners cut them down, and new wreckage appeared along the Aluminum Trail.

Like the Flying Tigers, the Fourteenth Air Force had its share of wartime heroes. Perhaps the best known was Casey Vincent, who became a brigadier general at the age of 29, the second youngest person to attain that rank since the Civil War. He also served as the model for Colonel Vince Casey, a character in Milton Caniff's comic strip *Terry and the Pirates*.

Just as the Flying Tigers had grown into a full-fledged air force, Chennault's old early warning network had not only remained active but also evolved into an effective intelligence organization. Lieutenant Colonel Wilfred Smith directed the information-gathering effort from Casey Vincent's headquarters at Kweilin. Most of Smith's field agents and all his administrators were Americans, some with missionary backgrounds. Their principal contacts apparently were westernized Chinese. Besides obtaining reports from these sources, the agents sometimes led downed airmen to safety and frequently doubled as forward air controllers, directing strikes by radio from the ground.

Wilfred Smith was himself the son of a missionary. One of his assistants, Major Paul Frillman, had operated a Lutheran mission at Hankow before the war, then served as a chaplain to the Flying Tigers. Lieutenant Robert Lynn had been a medical missionary, and Corporal Sven Liljestrand was a missionary's son. Among the exceptions that proved the rule were two agents who had not engaged in evangelism. One, Major Sam West, had been a salesman in the prewar Orient; the other, Captain Harold Rosholt, was formerly a newspaperman covering the Sino-Japanese conflict.

The most famous of Chennault's intelligence officers proved to be Captain John Birch, a Baptist missionary serving in China when war broke out between the United States and Japan. In April 1942, Birch came across Jimmy Doolittle and the crew of his B-25, who had parachuted over the mainland after bombing Japan, and led them to friendly lines. The young missionary then joined Chennault's intelligence service, establishing contact with guerrilla forces in the Yangtze valley, locating targets for air strikes and on one occasion sitting in the nose of a B-25 to point out an enemy ammunition dump to the bombardier. Birch refused a transfer to the Office of Strategic Services, and was serving with the Fourteenth Air Force at the time of his death. Just 10 days after the war had ended, while serving as a liaison officer with Nationalist forces, he was captured by a Communist patrol. When he demanded to be released, his captors became angry and shot him to death; a more conciliatory attitude might possibly have saved his life. Some years later, Robert Welch, a retired candy manufacturer, proclaimed Birch a martyr and established the ultraconservative John Birch Society.

John Birch, however, was not the only hero among Wilfred Smith's intelligence operatives. Paul Frillman, for example, had remained in the town of Changteh, surrounded by the Japanese, calling down air strikes on the approaching enemy until he made a last-minute nighttime escape. Sam West single-handedly broke up an attempted river crossing by Japanese forces, using his radio to direct bombing and strafing runs by the Chinese-American Composite Wing.

Meanwhile the warning net continued to function. Observers equipped with binoculars, who communicated with airfield command centers by radio or telephone, remained the principal means of alerting fighter units after the creation of the Fourteenth Air Force. Not until 1944 did radar for ground-controlled interception come into use in China. Colonel Winston Kratz, while visiting the combat theater to supervise the deployment of radar, expressed amazement that the Fourteenth Air Force operated a system of ground observers little changed from that which Chennault had devised for Air Corps maneuvers back in the 1930s. "The simple truth," Kratz decided, "is that this entire air force is terribly behind in air defense matters." Considering all that Chennault's fighter pilots had accomplished with this crude warning net, the remark was more tribute than criticism.

Along with the ground-control intercept radars, Fourteenth Air Force received a squadron of Northrop P-61A Black Widows. These massive twin-engine night fighters, which carried their own airborne radar, weighed more than the B-25Bs flown by the old China Air Task Force. The two-man Black Widow crew was housed in a pod located between the two booms that contained the 2,250-horsepower engines and extended aft of the wing to support the tail assembly. Armament consisted of four .50-caliber guns in a remote-controlled dorsal turret and four 20-mm cannon firing forward from the belly of the crew compartment.

On 30 October 1944, Captain Robert R. Scott (not to be confused with Colonel Robert L. Scott) scored the first radar-controlled victory of the China war. A ground station brought him within three miles of his intended victim, and the airborne radar operator then took over, guiding Scott close enough to see the Japanese bomber. The enemy caught sight of the Black Widow at almost the same instant, but Scott pursued his prey through a series of turns, staggering at times on the brink of a stall but finally getting off 240 rounds that set the hostile plane ablaze. Aerial combat had changed radically since those nights in 1942 when Johnny Alison, Ajax Baumler and Tex Hill had craned their necks to spot the engine exhaust from enemy bombers overhead.

With his rapidly expanding force and its new equipment, Chennault carried out the aerial campaign he had urged upon President Roosevelt. Eventually the resources at the general's disposal far exceeded the estimates he had offered when he presented his case before the President. Instead of 233 combat aircraft, he had roughly 500 fighters, 100 medium bombers and 70 heavy bombers as 1944 drew to a close. Although handicapped by recurring supply shortages, especially of fuel, the Fourteenth Air Force carried the war to the enemy, claiming the sinking of more than 200,000 tons of shipping by the end of 1943. Postwar evaluation, however, could verify the destruction of just one-fifth that amount. Confirming ship sinkings proved as difficult as verifying aerial kills. Through a curtain of bursting antiaircraft shells, small ships looked like large ones, merchantmen like warships and smokescreens or even normal funnel smoke like raging shipboard blazes.

Attacks on Japanese vessels continued, with some 700,000 tons claimed sunk during 1944. After one such raid, Major Horace Carswell remained at the controls of a damaged B-24 so that the crew members could take to their parachutes. After discovering that one man had a damaged parachute, he tried for a crash landing but hit a mountain side. The Army paid tribute to Carswell's heroism by the posthumous award of the Medal of Honor.

Although damage claims proved excessive—a usual result of the confusion and excitement of aerial combat—the Fourteenth Air Force was hurting the enemy. Yet Chennault soon found that his command would have to yield its priority on tonnage flown over the Hump. The recipient of these supplies was to be Project Matterhorn, an attempt to bomb Japan from bases in China.

Selected to carry out Matterhorn were the new Boeing B-29 Superfortresses. These bombers, which featured such refinements as remotely controlled gun turrets and pressurized cabins, could carry eight tons of bombs and had a maximum range in excess of 5,000 miles. This was the ultimate strategic bomber, and because of its devastating potential the Army Air Forces grouped all the B-29s in the specially created Twentieth Air Force. General Arnold, acting through a deputy, retained command of the new organization, which was under the operational control of the U.S. Joint Chiefs of Staff. The Twentieth Air Force would attack Japan both from central China and from airfields in the Marianas, once amphibious forces had seized those islands.

The principal role of the Fourteenth Air Force in Project Matterhorn was to supervise the construction of a series of air bases around the city of Chengtu and then help defend them against air attack. Hundreds of thousands of Chinese farmers, pressed into service by the governor of Szechwan province, drained rice paddies and built nine airfields, four of them with 9,000-foot runways, within 90 days. At each site the laborers fitted cobblestones into place to form the infrastructure and topped it off with crushed rock packed down with massive hand-drawn rollers. This engineering achievement, though essential to Matterhorn, weakened a Chinese economy already tottering on the brink of collapse. The diversion of land and labor from farming reduced the supply of rice and drove up its cost,

The general visits his pilots

while the infusion of millions of additional American dollars to pay for the work greatly increased currency inflation.

Even as the construction around Chengtu approached completion, Chennault complained to Arnold about the independent status of the XX Bomber Command, which was to operate from the new bases under the command of Brigadier General Kenneth Wolfe. The Fourteenth Air Force commander wanted control of the B-29s in the event the raids upon Japan provoked "really determined counter-operations" and it became necessary "to use their power to deliver an enormous weight of bombs, to pulverize Hankow or other major bases of a Japanese offensive." Indeed, Chennault was certain that the building of these vast airfields, which could only signify a plan to bomb Japan, would trigger a savage reaction. "Because they fear long range bombing in Japan," he warned Arnold, "I expect the Japanese to stage a major battle for air supremacy in China this spring . . ." The Commanding General, Army Air Forces, remained certain, however, that Matterhorn bombers should be controlled from Washington.

Actually, the enemy had already planned a limited offensive designed to consolidate his control over eastern China while eliminating the Fourteenth Air Force bases used to attack coastal shipping. Since Japanese air power had failed to defeat Chennault, the ground forces would attempt to overrun his bases. On 17 April 1944 the first phase began with an attack designed to pinch off a Chinese salient north of Hankow. An advance south

Special bases were built for the huge B-29s

from that city toward Hengyang was scheduled for June. Subsequent drives would overrun Kweilin and reach the Indochina border. For the time being, at least, Chengtu lay beyond the enemy's reach.

The offensive caught Chennault at an awkward time. Orders to protect the Chengtu airfields tied down some of his fighters, and fuel was scarce because Wolfe had begun stockpiling gasoline for his Matterhorn operations. Besides using Superfortresses to carry gasoline, the chief of the XX Bomber Command had to call upon C-46s, C-87s and C-109s that otherwise would have supported the Fourteenth Air Force. A future Secretary of Defense, Lieutenant Colonel Robert S. McNamara, who already was looked upon as a managerial wizard, took over the scheduling of the aerial tankers, and by summer enough gasoline was reaching Chengtu so that routine diversions from Chennault's command no longer were necessary.

The assurance of adequate fuel enabled the Fourteenth Air Force to delay the Japanese advance southward from Hankow. Chennault realized, however, that his airmen needed help and called upon Arnold to use the B-29s against Hankow, supply base and command center for the Japanese offensive. When Arnold refused, Chennault persuaded Lieutenant General Albert C. Wedemeyer, who had replaced the embattled Stilwell, to order XX Bomber Command into action. Upon receiving the theater commander's instructions, Major General Curtis E. LeMay, who had taken over from Wolfe, pointed out that the Joint Chiefs of Staff controlled his

Ground facilities at a Chinese base

bombers, but the service leaders endorsed Wedemeyer. As a result, during daylight on 18 December 1944, 84 Superfortresses dumped incendiary bombs on Hankow. Smoke and errors in scheduling a companion raid by Chennault's squadrons caused more than 60 percent of the bombs to fall outside the target area, but those that struck home caused fires that achieved almost 50 percent destruction.

Although devastating in effect, the Hankow raid did not stop the Japanese. By the end of February 1945, Chennault's units had been forced from eastern China. Although Chengtu remained in friendly hands, the Matterhorn project was approaching an inglorious end after bombing targets in Japan and throughout enemy-occupied Asia.

Despite prodding from Arnold, the China-based B-29s had accomplished little in comparison to the effort expended to keep them flying. Robert McNamara and his managerial team could not work miracles; after all, tankers flying the Hump had to burn almost two gallons of gasoline for every gallon delivered. On the eve of Trident, in the spring of 1943, General Arnold had complained that Chiang and Chennault were ignoring logistical realities in their plans to wage aerial war in China. But the commanding general had gone on to launch a more ambitious air campaign that required even greater stocks of fuel and supplies, and the same realities had frustrated his efforts. The last Matterhorn mission, an attack on Singapore, occurred on 29 March 1945. By this time, LeMay had assumed command of B-29 operations from the Marianas and abandoned high-altitude precision bombing for night incendiary raids that burned entire cities.

After overrunning Chennault's easternmost air bases, the Japanese paused to regroup. Mustangs of the 312th Fighter Wing, deployed with the B-29s to help protect the Chengtu airfields, now escorted Chennault's Liberators against rail lines and bridges that carried supplies for the enemy. By the end of March, however, Chennault decided that the B-24s burned too much fuel and sent them to India. Medium bombers and fighters maintained pressure on land and river transportation and continued attacking coastal shipping.

April saw the last effort by the Japanese, an attack westward from Hengyang that the Chinese easily contained. With enemy divisions already retreating toward North China for eventual redeployment to Japan, Chiang's armies reoccupied the airfields abandoned a few months earlier. In August, Marianas-based B-29s dropped atomic bombs on Hiroshima and Nagasaki; Japan, starved of oil and other critical war materials by marauding American submarines, agreed to surrender.

As the fighting drew to a close, General Wedemeyer carried out a reorganization of American forces in China that Chennault interpreted as an attempt by his superiors in Washington to get rid of him. This assess-

Japanese locomotives explode after strafing attack

ment may well have been correct, for Generals Marshall and Arnold had looked with disfavor upon his freewheeling disregard of command channels. Now that President Roosevelt, Chennault's principal supporter, was dead and China had become a secondary theater, they may have felt they could shelve this troublesome officer.

Rather than agree to shift his headquarters to Chengtu, now a backwater in an unimportant area of operations, Chennault submitted a request for retirement. On 31 July, Major General C. B. Stone, a newcomer to the Far East, took over the Fourteenth Air Force. After a final interview with Chiang and a triumphant tour of the cities his airmen had helped defend, Chennault boarded a departing C-47 on 8 August, two days after the Hiroshima raid.

"I left China full of anger and disappointment," Chennault later declared. "For eight long years my sole ambition was the defeat of the Japanese, and now I was deprived of participating in that final victory." Despite his undeniable contributions to Allied success—a Japanese general who commanded in central China acknowledged that "operations of the Fourteenth Air Force . . . constituted between 60 and 75 percent of our effective opposition in China"—Chennault was not among those present on the deck of the battleship USS *Missouri*, when Japan formally surrendered.

# 13. Chennault and His Flying Tigers: A Summing Up

The Flying Tigers made both a moral and a military contribution to victory over Japan. In the discouraging months that followed Pearl Harbor, the enemy overran Hong Kong, Malaya, the Netherlands East Indies, the Philippines and Burma. Only the aerial victories of Scarsdale Jack Newkirk and the other volunteers sustained Allied morale at this critical time, offering proof that the Japanese could be beaten.

Besides providing hope in a time of despair, the American Volunteer Group taught a lesson in tactics, showing other fliers exactly how to defeat the Zero fighter. Early warning, the use of two-man fighting teams, diving to take advantage of sturdier aircraft, firing accurately with heavy machine guns—this became the standard formula by which heavier American planes could shoot down the nimbler Japanese. Leaders like Pappy Boyington learned how to pit the strong points of their fighters against the enemy's weaknesses and taught the lesson to others.

In winning their aerial victories, the American Volunteer Group excited the press and public, although their swaggering style dismayed the more conventional military authorities. While defending Rangoon, the Flying Tigers made a barroom their headquarters and found time between aerial battles to brawl with British soldiers, defy the colonial caste system and even fight with an occasional civilian. Yet once the Tigers were aloft, they dropped this air of recklessness, fighting in disciplined two-man teams; only in desperate circumstances, such as being caught on the ground by Japanese bombers, did any of them climb into battle without a wingman.

In short, the group was a collection of individuals, driven by various combinations of motives, ranging from financial gain to selfless patriotism. The Flying Tigers were living contradictions. A professed cynic like Boyington risked his neck to recover aircraft that had crash-landed through what he considered his own carelessness. These self-styled mercenaries could be as sentimental toward each other as they were deadly in combat. Bob Neale, credited with downing 15.50 Japanese planes, cried when he said good-bye to his commander. John Petach responded to Chennault's appeal for help by remaining in China after his contract had expired and sacrificing his life in an attempt to teach newcomers what he had learned about aerial combat as a Flying Tiger.

Although the Chinese government agreed to pay a bonus for planes destroyed on the ground, the Tigers detested strafing missions, despite the lure of profit. The danger seemed too great, for they had to yield the altitude advantage and seldom had planes enough to provide fighter cover for the pilots making the attacks. Mercenaries they may have been, but the combination of fatigue and danger overcame the promise of money and drove them to the point of mutiny. Veteran leaders prevailed, however, appealing mainly to pride and patriotism, and most of the Flying Tigers agreed to gamble their lives against formidable odds.

Contributing to this near rebellion, and possibly to the boisterous camaraderie among the pilots, was a sense of neglect and isolation. Almost to a man, the Flying Tigers believed they had been abandoned by the United States government to fight in an alien land against a better-equipped and better-supplied enemy. Everything they needed, from gasoline to chocolate bars, had to travel halfway around the world and, as a result, was always in short supply. These circumstances bred a kind of angry pride in doing the job with cast-off equipment, in triumphing over the indifference of those who should be looking out for them.

The aircraft warning net upon which the Flying Tigers depended served as an example both of isolation and of the response it engendered. The standard tool of air defense, radar, did not become available in China until the B-29s put in their appearance. Yet for almost three years the volunteer group and its successors won impressive victories with the kind of warning net that Chennault had organized before Pearl Harbor.

Pilots in the American Volunteer Group had little use for staff officers, their own included. This feeling stemmed in part from the natural contempt of aviator toward nonflier, but many of the organization's staff specialists were amateurs. The Army Air Corps, short of officers with staff

American bombing supports Chinese ground operations

training or experience, had refused to make any of them available to the Flying Tigers.

Poor staff work, in fact, became a hallmark of both the China Air Task Force and the Fourteenth Air Force. Probably because of his experience with the Flying Tigers, Chennault tended to be his own director of plans and chief of intelligence. When talented staff officers began arriving, they could not make the contribution they should have made. Their commander prized willingness to work long hours and to take part in combat missions more than he valued skill at marshaling facts and drawing sound conclusions.

The China Air Task Force and Fourteenth Air Force inherited other characteristics from the Flying Tigers. Airmen serving in China tended to ignore the trappings of military life; indeed, Chennault himself arrived in Washington on the eve of the Trident conference without a proper uniform. In contrast to this sloppiness, the successors to the volunteer group insisted on precise discipline in the air. Men like Tex Hill, Frank Schiel, Ed Rector, Robert L. Scott and Bob Neale stressed the importance of teamwork, while John Hampshire, James England and Pappy Herbst proved both apt pupils and excellent teachers in their own right.

Another trait common to the organizations descended from the Flying Tigers was the persisting sense of insecurity, the realization that at any moment essential supplies could be diverted elsewhere. Rare was the individual who did not at some time feel bitter toward higher authority. Professional officers like Casey Vincent tried to remain aloof, however, realizing that friction among major commanders could delay the defeat of Japan.

The Flying Tigers, the China Air Task Force and the Fourteenth Air Force were the handiwork of one man, Claire L. Chennault. Immediately after the war he obtained a divorce and married Anna Chan, a journalist whom he had met in China. Anna Chennault always maintained that her husband had performed two wartime miracles. Creation of the American Volunteer Group was the first; the second was establishment of the Fourteenth Air Force. Her assessment was correct, inasmuch as no one but Claire Chennault could have held the Flying Tigers together or gained approval for a full-fledged air force in China.

Chennault, however, had been reluctant to attempt the first miracle. The record of the International Squadron did not inspire confidence in foreign airmen, even though Jim Allison and George Weigle had shown both courage and skill. When Chiang decided to hire fighter pilots to hold off the Japanese until Chinese squadrons could be organized, equipped and trained, Chennault tackled the job with his usual zeal, convincing Thomas Corcoran, friend and adviser to President Roosevelt, that the United States government should support the undertaking.

Chennault with General Albert C. Wedemeyer

Once the President had unofficially encouraged military pilots to volunteer for service in China, Chennault left the actual recruiting to others, but he soon placed his personal stamp on the organization. He lectured his men on tactics, taught them the weaknesses of every type of Japanese warplane and patiently corrected their errors. In handling his contract pilots, he avoided issuing peremptory commands he could not enforce and consulted with his senior pilots before meting out punishment. His disciplinary choices actually were few; he could fire an individual, the equivalent of a dishonorable discharge, or impose fines for misconduct. In either case, his action had to reflect the collective judgment of the group, if good order was to be preserved.

During the months between his return to active duty in April 1942 and the formation of the China Air Task Force in July, Chennault in theory could issue orders backed by the authority of his rank and enforceable by courts-martial. In practice, as he realized, he depended upon the cooperation of men whose contracts were about to expire, and he therefore had no more power than before. When crises arose, he wisely relied on persuasion, his own and that of squadron leaders like Tex Hill.

Chennault was a master of persuasion. Even Boyington, who prided himself on being able to spot a phony, found the general impressive. The marine especially admired two things about the group commander. One was Chennault's ability to forge individuals into a fighting team, a talent that Boyington shared; the other was the way young women flocked around the older airman.

Thomas Corcoran, who told President Roosevelt that Chennault was "the most original brass" he had ever met, became a friend of the general. Tommy the Cork once compared the leader of the Flying Tigers to T. E. Lawrence, the British soldier-scholar who during World War I had led the Arabs to victory over their Turkish rulers. "Each," the Washington attorney declared, "spectacularly fought imaginative 'open' and, most importantly, guerrilla wars—Lawrence's Bedouins on camels striking from the desert, Chennault's fighter planes hopping hit-and-run from one abandoned airfield to another." Although both these military leaders were innovators, the analogy was false. Lawrence encouraged his desert guerrillas to attack Turkish lines of communication; in China, however, it was Chennault who depended upon a supply line vulnerable not only to enemy action but also to senior commanders who might divert cargo to meet the needs of other theaters. The fact that every drop of fuel burned in China had to be imported by air restricted the courses of action open to Chennault. He could not use machines to wage the kind of mobile, irregular campaign that Lawrence had directed in the desert.

Chennault's second miracle, the Fourteenth Air Force, was the result of his powers of persuasion, his confidence in himself and his men and his willingness to defy military protocol. The accomplishments of the Flying

Chiang honors Chennault at a farewell
dinner

Tigers, confirmed by the success of the China Air Task Force, convinced him that an aerial offensive launched in China would bring Japan to its knees. Once he had fixed upon this goal, he devoted all his energy to achieving it.

Anyone who raised objections to his plan became Chennault's enemy. Chiang, for his own reasons, endorsed the idea, thus confirming Chennault's high opinion of the Generalissimo. With Joseph Alsop's help, the Fourteenth Air Force commander sold his strategy to President Roosevelt, but not everyone succumbed to his rhetoric. Those who remained unmoved—Stilwell, Arnold and Marshall—joined the list of enemies. Ever since his days at the Air Corps Tactical School, Chennault had tended to interpret honest disagreement as an attack on his integrity, reacting accordingly. This sensitiveness to criticism triggered feuds, like his quarrel with Bissell, that lasted for years.

The aerial campaign for which Chennault had such hopes not only failed to defeat the Japanese but helped prod them into action. As Stilwell had suggested, the enemy, stung by air power, had reacted on the ground. The Army general summarized Chennault's problem in bitter terms. The airman, he declared, had "assured the Generalissimo that air power is the answer." Because of the Japanese reaction, Stilwell continued, Chennault had come to realize his error and was trying "to duck the consequences of having sold the wrong bill of goods" by shifting the blame to "those who pointed out the danger long ago . . ." Resentment at having the ground war sacrificed on the altar of air power lent an edge to these words, but the fact remained that Chennault had been wrong. He realized that a ground war could be lost in the air, but he overlooked the possibility that the air war might be lost on the ground.

Many of Chennault's problems stemmed from his confidence in Chiang Kai-shek, who seemed to him the embodiment of China. When the Nationalist leader promised to defend the airfields of eastern China, this pledge satisfied the American airman. He apparently failed to see that the Generalissimo might undertake almost any commitment to rid himself of Stilwell, who kept demanding action on the ground, so that a reinforced Fourteenth Air Force could fight China's war with American resources. Moreover, when the Japanese overran these bases, Chennault absolved Chiang, instead blaming his enemies within the armed forces for not supporting him adequately.

In short, Chennault's obsession with air power, his difficulty in getting along with superiors and his tendency to overreact to criticism combined to prevent him from being a truly successful general. He was, however, a brilliant leader of men, teaching them patiently and inspiring them to triumph over impossible odds. He proved himself a great captain, a 20th-century *condottiere*, the brain and heart of the Flying Tigers. Thus did he contribute to victory.

# 14. An End to Miracles

Chennault's accomplishments did not end with the war. Miracle number three, the founding of China Air Transport, dated from New Year's Day, 1946, when he landed at Shanghai. As he journeyed inland, following the Yangtze River, he saw at first hand the destruction caused by the conflict. Scarcely a single rat remained in a city the size of Hankow, for the starving citizens had caught and eaten them. Boiled weeds, tree bark and straw replaced rice in the Chinese diet. Oxen and water buffalo had either been confiscated by the Japanese or killed for food by their owners after the fighting ended. "Families yoked themselves in buffalo harness, and tried to drag heavy wooden plows and harrows through thick rice-paddy mud," he reported, "but their half-starved bodies were unequal to the task."

The United Nations Relief and Rehabilitation Administration was shipping food to China, but these supplies could not get beyond the seaports. Chennault's airmen had been too accurate in shooting up trucks, bombing bridges and severing rail lines; except for porters, an occasional oxcart and a few surviving river craft like the one carrying the retired general, nothing was moving toward the nation's interior. To Chennault, the solution lay in air transport, but only a few dozen war-weary C-47s were available to haul the relief supplies. The newer cargo planes provided by the United States were working full time to deliver munitions and supplies to Nationalist forces fighting the Chinese Communists.

Most of the civil aircraft were the property of China National Airways Corporation. In existence since the 1930s, this organization had been a model of improvisation as it flew cargo, passengers and even farm animals throughout Nationalist-held China. For instance, when Japanese bombs shattered the wing of a parked DC-2, mechanics replaced the ruined panel with one from the larger DC-3. After bolting the longer span in place, the ground crew christened their lopsided product a DC2½ and watched it take to the air.

When the Flying Tigers disbanded in July 1942, several members of the group stayed on at least temporarily as pilots for the Chinese air line. Among them were Bob Prescott, Dick Rossi, Bill Bartling, Catfish Raines, Joe Rosbert and Link Laughlin. The length of their service with this wing-and-a-prayer outfit varied, with some of them choosing to join the American armed forces. Combat, after all, could not have seemed more danger-ous than flying C-47s or C-46s in and out of rice paddies hastily converted into airstrips. Bartling and Laughlin, for example, tried one day to coax their overloaded C-46 into the air but ran out of room before the wheels left the ground. The plane tore through a grove of trees, barely missing a home occupied by a peasant family, and crunched to a stop. The fuel tanks burst, sending gasoline cascading over the wreckage, but someone from the nearby hut climbed into the shattered fuselage and dragged the crewmen to safety before fire broke out and consumed the aircraft.

An estimated 35,000 hours of flying the Hump, plus domestic flights in China, took a toll in men and equipment. Joe Rosbert and his copilot en-countered rapid icing, crashed against a Himalayan peak but miraculously survived; others were not so fortunate. Many planes and crews simply disappeared, and by the end of the war the surviving men were exhausted and the aircraft barely flyable. Currency inflation finished the attrition which the wartime operations had begun, as the cost of fuel, spare parts and replacement aircraft spiraled upward. At the time of Chennault's re-turn, abandoned airfields dotted China, but civil aircraft were not available to serve them.

The former leader of the American Volunteer Group talked with United Nations relief officials in China, persuading them that he should es-tablish a new airline for delivering food and medicine throughout China. During a hurried visit to the United States, he convinced Fiorello LaGuar-dia, the former mayor of New York City who now headed the relief ad-ministration, to award the new line a contract to distribute the food that clogged China's seaports. To help him fulfill this contract, Chennault ob-tained an experienced manager, Whiting Willaeur, who had served with China Defense Supplies, Inc., during Flying Tiger days and later gone to China as an American foreign aid official. The two men then borrowed enough money to equip their air line, which came to be called Civil Air Transport, with 19 surplus airplanes and to hire a group of war veterans, some of them former Flying Tigers, to operate and maintain them.

Meanwhile, several other men who had flown in the American Volunteer Group also were trying to set up an air line. The idea originated with Bob Prescott, who had hoped to buy a couple of surplus transports and fly cargo in Mexico. He enlisted the financial backing of Sam Mosher, who had helped organize the California Fruit Growers Association before entering the oil business. When he joined forces with Prescott, Mosher was thinking in terms of flying fruit, flowers and vegetables from California to cities in the East. Dick Rossi, Duke Hedman, Bill Bartling, Catfish Raines and other former Tigers, some of whom had flown with Prescott for China National Airways Corporation, invested their money and talents, and Prescott began shopping for airplanes.

Available at the time were 14 Budd Conestogas, twin-engine cargo planes, built of spot-welded stainless steel by a firm that normally produced railroad cars. The aircraft, in fact, resembled a winged passenger coach in general shape, although it actually served as an aerial freight car. The interior could hold two dozen persons on uncomfortable bucket seats, but the usual load was five tons of cargo that entered by means of a ramp at the rear of the compartment. These ungainly craft made up the original fleet of The National Skyway Freight Company, The Line of the Flying Tiger. In August 1946 one of the Budds landed at Atlanta with a load of California grapes, and the Flying Tiger Line, the organization's eventual title, was on its way to becoming a worldwide carrier of cargo and charter passengers.

Chennault's Civil Air Transport delivered its first load of cargo in January 1947, and by April 1948 the line was flying 2 million ton-miles per month. Relief supplies made up about 70 percent of the total volume, though the transports managed to load some paying cargo for return flights to the port cities. The payroll soon reached 1,100 employees, 850 of them Chinese; most of the pilots continued to be Americans.

To speed the recovery of Chinese agriculture, the air line flew seeds, cows and sheep to the farming regions. Truck parts and tires made up much of the tonnage when Chinese officials tried to restore highway traffic in the interior. Because of the soaring inflation, cargo manifests sometimes listed box after box of freshly printed currency, which might decline in value during the course of the flight. Although purchasing power kept eroding, trade began making a comeback, and Civil Air Transport planes took on silk, tea, tobacco, cotton and other export goods.

The civil war between Communists and Nationalists, which Chiang had been anticipating for years, put an end to economic recovery and forced Chennault's air line to become increasingly involved in the support of military operations. During the six-month siege of Mukden, Manchuria,

**167**

Anna Chennault kept Americans
reminded of her husband's
accomplishments

Civil Air Transport delivered thousands of tons of food, medicine and other supplies. On their return flights, the transports brought out noncombatants and wounded soldiers. Mukden, however, fell to the Communists, and fighting spread throughout the region.

Manchuria soon became a vast trap for entire Nationalist armies, flown there by American airmen and then supplied mainly by Civil Air Transport. At one time, Chennault's crews were flying 50 missions a day into hurriedly built airfields, frequently braving artillery fire to land desperately needed cargo. After losing Manchuria and northern China, Nationalist remnants retreated to the Canton area, to Hainan Island and eventually to Taiwan, where Chiang Kai-shek established his government.

Chennault moved his airline to Taiwan, and there it prospered. Within a decade, Civil Air Transport had begun service all along the perimeter of Asia from South Korea to South Vietnam. Like the Nationalist cause, the airline had survived the Communist conquest of the mainland; the 19 transports that began hauling relief supplies in 1947 evolved into an international organization.

During this period of growth, Chennault's company remained involved in the continuing struggle with Asian Communism. When Communist North Korea invaded South Korea in 1950, Civil Air Transport flew passengers and cargo in support of the American forces fighting there. Almost four years later, when the Communist Viet Minh surrounded the French garrison at Dien Bien Phu in Indochina, Chennault's airmen again saw service.

Using Fairchild Flying Boxcars made available by the U.S. Air Force, volunteer air crews from Civil Air Transport parachuted supplies to the embattled French. One of these volunteers was James McGovern, a bearded, muscular American, nicknamed "Earthquake McGoon" after a villainous hillbilly in Al Capp's comic strip *Li'l Abner*. Six tons of ammunition waited on pallets to be pushed from the cargo compartment of McGovern's plane, when a shell from a Russian-built 37-mm gun knocked out one of his engines. McGovern and his copilot, Wallace Buford, continued toward the drop zone, until another shell tore into one of the booms that supported the tail surfaces. The Flying Boxcar immediately began losing altitude, but McGovern, Buford and the French cargo handlers that completed the crew stayed with the doomed plane to keep the ammunition from detonating among troops they had been trying to supply. The loaded pallets remained in place, as the aircraft limped beyond the encircled French bastion. "It looks like this is it," said McGovern to Buford. These were the last words heard over the open microphone, for seconds later the transport struck a ridge and exploded.

The Viet Minh victory over the French in Indochina inspired Chennault to attempt a fourth miracle. He began sounding out his contacts in the United States and on Taiwan, investigating the possibility of forming an

On course: B-24 Liberators wing their
way toward the enemy

international volunteer group to help defend Laos and South Vietnam. Before the project could take shape, death intervened; on 27 July 1958 cancer took the life of Claire L. Chennault.

In his tribute to Chennault, Joseph Alsop called him "the old hero." Thomas Corcoran urged that people forget the quarrels in which the general had engaged and remember the "courage, skill, and devotion . . . of a commander who, his peers say, did more with less than any American commander of the war." Anna Chennault reminded Americans of the accomplishments of "a man whose face, name, and famous deeds had caught the imagination of the entire world: the greatest Flying Tiger of them all, Chennault of China."

# In Context

In *Tigers Over Asia*, we have seen how war came to China. Sometimes, in fact, it is said that World War II really began in the summer of 1937, when the Japanese resumed their drive on the Asian mainland. But the generally accepted date for the start of the war is 1 September 1939, the day when the Germany of Adolf Hitler launched its invasion of Poland. It was a quick, victorious campaign for the German armies. And, in 1940, while Japan pursued her goals in China, the Germans swept through western Europe in an amazing march of conquest: Denmark, Norway, the Netherlands, Luxembourg, Belgium and, to the world's shock, France. But the Germans could not march across water; they could not conquer Britain without control of the air and thus of the sea. This control the Battle of Britain, fought in the summer of 1940, denied them. The war in Europe would go on.

The United States eyed the astonishing German successes with deep apprehension. Nor was Germany the only source of concern for America, as this book has made plain. President Roosevelt and his advisers viewed Japan's attempts to establish the "Greater East Asia Co-Prosperity Sphere"—the extension of the Japanese Empire to Burma, Indochina, Malaya and the Netherlands East Indies—as a threat to American security.

The Axis partners—Germany, Italy and Japan—seemed to be riding the wave of victory as 1941 unfolded. But the great German invasion of the Soviet Union was stopped at the gates of Moscow, and in this same December came the Japanese attack on Pearl Harbor—bringing the United States into alliance with Britain and Russia against the Axis.

In accordance with previously agreed-upon strategy, the main American effort was first directed against Germany—considered the heart of the Axis alliance. The Pacific was not ignored, of course. Great and continuing efforts were made along supply lines that strained logistical facilities. And with surprising speed the Americans won a strategic victory in the Battle of the Coral Sea in May 1942 and a month later followed up with the pivotal, tide-turning triumph at Midway. The United States could now take the offensive in the Pacific, as is demonstrated in the Men and Battle book entitled *Carrier Victory*. Islands would be won that could provide bases for bombing attacks on the Japanese Home Islands. As this book has shown, attempts to bomb Japan from Chinese bases met with failure. The final phase of the Pacific war is described in another book in this series, *Okinawa: The Great Island Battle*.

Meanwhile, the Anglo-American allies, in 1942 and 1943, carried the war to Northwest Africa and then across the Mediterranean by way of Sicily to Italy—a complete victory having been won in Africa, from Cairo to Casablanca. While the American amphibious forces moved closer and closer to Japan itself, the Allies plunged into Europe at the Normandy beaches, as the Soviets drove the Germans back from the east. The Germans could only delay the outcome. They could not change it. The war in Europe did not end in 1944, as many had hoped, but by the spring of 1945 Nazi Germany was in ruins and Hitler dead. Japan, thanks principally to American possession of the atomic bomb, had little more than three months to go.

# For Further Reading

BOYINGTON, GREGORY. *Baa Baa Black Sheep.* New York: Bantam Books, 1958.
    A rich vein of war stories, edged in cynicism.
CHENNAULT, ANNA. *Chennault and the Flying Tigers.* New York: Paul S. Eriksson, 1963.
    Adds interesting detail to the account in *Way of a Fighter* (see below).
CRAVEN, WESLEY FRANK, and CATE, JAMES LEA. (eds). *Plans and Early Operations* (The Army Air Forces in World War II series). Chicago: University of Chicago Press, 1948.
    This volume, along with Volumes IV and V, contains the official account of the China Air Task Force and the Fourteenth Air Force.
————. *The Pacific: Guadalcanal to Saipan* (The Army Air Forces in World War II series). Chicago: University of Chicago Press, 1950.
————. *The Pacific: Matterhorn to Nagasaki* (The Army Air Forces in World War II series). Chicago: University of Chicago Press, 1953.
————. *Services Around the World* (The Army Air Forces in World War II series). Chicago: University of Chicago Press, 1958.
    Contains excellent accounts of the India-China airlift and the building of B-29 bases in China.
HOTZ, ROBERT, ed. *Way of a Fighter: The Memoirs of Claire Lee Chennault.* New York: G. P. Putnam's Sons, 1949.
    A fascinating book in which the subject presents himself warts and all.

**175**

MCCLURE, GLENN E. *Fire and Fall Back*. Universal City, Tex., 1975.

Described as the book that Casey Vincent would have written, had he not died suddenly of a heart attack, it contains his diary and extracts from some letters.

PENTECOST, WALTER E., and SLOAN, JAMES J. "Advance of the Flying Tigers," *Journal of the American Aviation Historical Society*, Summer, 1970, pp. 137–144.

An account of the assembly of the American Volunteer Group's Curtiss P-40B fighters.

ROMANUS, CHARLES F., and SUNDERLAND, RILEY. *Stilwell's Mission to China*. Washington: Office of the Chief of Military History, 1953.

Official history at its best, this is the first of three excellent volumes that provide a thorough and generally balanced account of the Stilwell-Chennault controversy and the conduct of Chennault's air campaign.

———. *Stilwell's Command Problems*. Washington: Office of the Chief of Military History, 1956.

———. *Time Runs Out in CBI*. Washington: Office of the Chief of Military History, 1959.

SCOTT, ROBERT L. *Flying Tiger: Chennault of China*. Garden City, N.Y.: Doubleday, 1959.

A tribute to the general, written not long after his death by a veteran of the China air war.

———. *God Is My Co-Pilot*. New York: Charles Scribner's Sons, 1943.

A personal memoir dealing in part with the American Volunteer Group and the China Air Task Force.

TUCHMAN, BARBARA W. *Stilwell and the American Experience in China, 1911–1945*. New York: Macmillan, 1970.

Stilwell is the hero and Chennault a villain in this brilliantly written book.

WAGNER, RAY. "The Chinese Air Force, 1931–1940," *Journal of the American Aviation Historical Society*, Fall 1974, pp. 162–171.

Essential background to the story of the Flying Tigers.

WHELAN, RUSSELL. *The Flying Tigers*. New York: Warner Paperback Library, 1972.

A reprint of a wartime account, filled with anecdotes.

# Index

**177**

**179**

North American B-25, 100, 111, 128
North American P-51 Mustang, 144-145
Northrop P-61 Black Widow, 144, 148
Northrop 2EC, 22

Office of Strategic Services (OSS), 88, 119
Older, Charles, 65, 67, 107, 146
Olson, Arvid, 64, 69, 70, 89, 94, 96
Overend, Ed, 65, 68, 69

Page, George, 137
Pan American Airways, 43, 106
*Panay* incident, 32
Panda Bears, *see* Flying Tigers
Pawley, Edwin, 33
Pawley, William, 26, 33, 65, 68-69
Pawley brothers, 33, 38, 46, 48
Pearl Harbor, 60, 157
Pensacola Naval Air Station, 42
Pentecost, Walter, 48
Petach, John, 77, 106-107, 111, 127
Polikarpov, Nikolai, 24
Polikarpov I-15, 24-25, 27
Polikarpov I-16, 24-25, 27, 28, 35
Porter, John F. ("Blackie"), 139
Prescott, Bob, 107, 166, 167
Prevo, Sam, 49
Project Matterhorn, 149-155
pursuit planes:
    controversy of bombers vs., 10-14
    tactics of, 1-4, 10-14, 23, 92, 157

Quadrant conference (Quebec, 1943), 136

radar, use of, 61, 148
Raines, R. J. ("Catfish"), 92, 108, 166, 167
Rangoon, 46, 48, 50, 52, 55, 61, 73, 78-79, 85
    Japanese bombing of, 64-80
Rector, Ed, 3, 64, 72, 87, 92, 96, 106, 107, 110,
    127, 159
Red Air Force, 24, 25-26, 27
Reed, Bill, 85, 107, 108, 146
Republic, 35
Republic P-43 Lancer, 36, 111
Republic P-47 Thunderbolt, 144
Reynolds, Thomas A., 146
Rice, Raymond, 144-145
Richards, Lewis, 49, 86
*Role of Defensive Pursuit, The* (Chennault),
    10-11
Rolls-Royce Merlin engine, 144
Roosevelt, Franklin D., 32-33, 34, 39, 92, 100,
    119-120, 122, 126, 129-130, 132, 133-134,
    135, 148, 156
Rosbert, Joe, 166
Rosholt, Harold, 147
Rossi, Dick, 87, 107, 166, 167
Royal Air Force, 33, 57, 64, 70, 76, 78, 85, 87
Russo-Japanese agreement (1941), 35

Sakagawa, Tosho, 143-144
Salween River, 79, 95-97, 124
Sandell, Robert, 3-4, 64, 70, 78, 107
Sawyer, Charley, 106, 127
Schiel, Frank, 92, 97, 106, 107, 110, 111, 127,
    146, 159

Schmued, Edgar, 145
Scott, Robert L., 104, 113, 115, 118, 122, 146,
    159
Scott, Robert R., 148
Seiple, Bill, 86
Sevareid, Eric, 139
Shamblin, Arnold, 111, 127
Shanghai, 17, 19, 22, 23, 132
Shilling, Erikson, 57, 64, 96
Silver Bar, 50, 73, 75
Singapore, 57
Smith, Curtis, 42, 46
Smith, Robert, 65, 67, 107
Smith, R. T. ("Snuffy"), 80, 96, 107
Smith, Wilfred, 147-148
Soong, T. V., 31-32, 33, 100, 101, 130
South China Sea, 132
Soviet Union, *see* China; Chinese Air Force;
    Red Air Force
Spanish influenza epidemic (1918), 7
Spitfire, 36
Stace, Don, 9
Stalin, Joseph, 24, 35
State Department, U.S., 43
Stevenson, D. F., 78
Stewart, Josephine, 46
Stilwell, Joseph W., 32, 93, 95, 126, 153
    Burma plans of, 119, 135-136
    Chennault and, 99, 101-102, 105, 118-121,
        129-130, 132-134, 139-140
    Chiang and, 19, 101, 122, 134, 164
    in ground war vs. air power controversy,
        101-102, 120, 133-135
    personality of, 133-134
Stimson, Henry L., 40, 132, 141
Stone, C. B., 156
Swartz, Frank, 86

Tak airfield, 74, 76, 77
Tenth Air Force, 99-100
    Flying Tigers and, 104-106, 110
*Terry and the Pirates,* 147
Thailand, 61-62, 74, 78, 87
"Three Men on a Flying Trapeze," 14-15, 16
Tien Ho, 125
Tonkin Gulf, 126, 143
Toungoo, 46, 49, 50-60, 61, 64
Towers, John, 39-40
Trident conference (Washington, 1943), 129,
    130, 135, 136, 139, 154
Trumble, Tom, 41-42, 56
Tunner, William H., 139
Tupolev SB-2, 24, 26, 35, 96
Twentieth Air Force, 149
XX Bomber Command, 152-154

United Nations Relief and Rehabilitation Ad-
    ministration, 165

Viet Minh, 170
Vincent, Clinton D. ("Casey"), 113-115, 118,
    142, 147, 160
Vultee, 35
Vultee P-48, 36
Vultee V-11, 26, 33